We Will Not Be Silenced

The Lived Experience of Sexual Harassment and Sexual Assault Told Powerfully Through Poetry, Prose, Essay, and Art

INDIE BLU(E)

PUBLISHING

We Will Not Be Silenced: The Lived Experience of Sexual
Harassment and Sexual Assault Told Powerfully Through Poetry,
Prose, Essay, and Art

For information, address
Indie Blu(e) Publishing
indieblucollective@gmail.com

Published in the United States of America
by Indie Blu(e) Publishing

ISBN: 978-1-7328000-0-7
Library of Congress Control Number: 2018913952

Editors: Christine E. Ray
                  Kindra M. Austin
                  Candice Louisa Daquin
                  Rachel Finch

Praise for *We Will Not Be Silenced*

'We Will Not be Silenced' is a call to arms; it is muffled voices upon strangled voices ripping the gags off to scream their stories and speak truth to power. *'We Will Not be Silenced'* is rage and heartbreak, it is the soul-crushing pain of the worst kind of human violation being laid bare for all to see, and it is laid bare with an unflinching power that demands you to keep reading. These stories are poignant and disturbing, and they are filled with everything this world needs to read right now. . .

'We Will Not Be Silenced' is a beautiful collection of devastating pieces, it is a siren call to survivors everywhere, and a book that should be showcased in every school, stocked on the shelves of every hospital, and sitting on the counters in every police station in the world. *'We Will Not Be Silenced'* should simply be available to everyone and anyone who has ever been violated, and to everyone and anyone who would be brave enough to speak out and speak up in an era when victims still aren't being heard.

Bravo to the fearless writers, poets, artists and survivors who shared their story in order to change the world. We hear you, and I know you hear us too.

- Nicole Lyons, *Blossom and Bone*

4

Dedication

In honor of all who screamed in vain...
For the memory of those who were long silenced...
With love for the ones who have no voice...
By those of us who are privileged to be heard,
This book is lovingly dedicated.

Acknowledgements

The Editors would like to thank the following:

The Bruised But Not Broken, Blood Into Ink, and Whisper and the Roar on-line communities for embracing this project and assisting with the Call for Submissions

Merril D. Smith for writing the Foreword for the book and setting it skillfully in historical and political context

RAINN for the daily support provided to survivors of sexual assault and for the resource information found in the back of the book

Grace Alexander for penning the perfect wording for the book's Dedication

Allane Sinclair for assisting the editors in creating a visual aesthetic for the book and for creating many of the graphic poetry pieces

Nicole Lyons and Jenny McKaig for graciously agreeing to reading drafts of the manuscript and writing advanced reviews

The Contributors would like to thank the following:

Thanks to our daughters and sons for giving us thousands of reasons to break the silence.

Rachael Ikins: I would also like to thank Bill Berry Jr. of Aaduna.org and co-organizer of Word Revisited for his support and faith in my work

Marilyn Rea Beyer: Salem Writers Group deserve immeasurable thanks for providing inspiration and creative room for all comers to bring ideas to the page.

Marilyn Rea Beyer: From the deepest well of my gratitude, thanks to Bobbie and Andy for giving me a sense of purpose and the strength to break my own silence.

Suzette Bishop: Thank you to Jackson MacKenzie for his book, *Psychopath Free: Recovering from Emotionally Abusive Relationships With Narcissists, Sociopaths, and Other Toxic People,* and the safe space to tell my story at *psychopathfree*.

Grace Alexander: With thanks always to Amanda, my sweetheart.

Table of Contents

17

kkc

20

Foreword
Merril D. Smith

"Brett's assault on me drastically altered my life."
Christine Blasey Ford (Ford 2018)

Survivors of sexual harassment, abuse, and assault are marked forever by their experiences. Though circumstances vary, survivors may endure bruises both to their bodies and souls, complicated by anxiety, fear, and shame. Often, they think they will not be believed if they tell, or they fear retaliation for doing so.

Moreover, in the United States and throughout the world, there are still many myths about both sexual assault and how victims should behave. As well as being blamed for using alcohol or drugs, wearing "provocative" attire, or being in a particular place at a particular time, women and girls are victimized again if they do not behave as some expect them to behave when attacked or following an assault. Psychology professor Kevin Michael Swartout has noted "research indicates that people are less likely to believe a victim's account and believe an assault was less severe when the assault and victim's response doesn't follow people's scripts" (Murphy, 2018).

Tarana Burke coined the phrase "Me Too" in 2006 as a way of giving victims of sexual harassment and violence a voice. In October 2017, following accusations of sexual assault against Hollywood producer Harvey Weinstein, actress Alyssa Milano tweeted a suggestion that all women who had been sexually harassed or abused should post their status using #MeToo." Milano later publicly credited Burke for the phrase and campaign. The slogan has become the phrase of a world-wide movement against sexual harassment and violence toward women. Though the "Me Too" movement sparked both awareness and activism, Christine Blasey Ford's allegations in that Supreme Court nominee Brett Kavanaugh sexually assaulted her when they were both in high school- and their subsequent testimony-

roused survivors of sexual assault in unprecedented numbers. The Rape, Abuse, & Incest National Network (RAINN) reported that calls to their National Sexual Assault Hotline increased by 738% during the testimony in September 2018. "This story has clearly resonated with survivors, and has led thousands to reach out for help for the first time," RAINN President Scott Berkowitz said in a statement. "Over this past year, following the cases of [Harvey] Weinstein and [Bill] Cosby and the explosion of #MeToo, our numbers have been growing pretty rapidly, but we've never seen anything like this before" (Fang 2018). CSPAN also received numerous calls from viewers who revealed their own stories of sexual assault, sometimes for the first time.

For example, seventy-six-year-old Brenda called to say how hearing Ford recount her experience brought back her own memory of being sexually assaulted when she was in second grade. "I thought it was over. But it's not. You will never forget it," she said (Miller 2018). The constant of sexual violence in the lives of women and girls has been amply and unfortunately revealed to me in my research, but the realization was recently brought closer to home. Knowing of my work and inspired by the Me Too movement, three women at the local gym I belong to have confided to me their rape stories. Two of the women never reported their assaults, which happened decades ago. The third woman reported her recent rape immediately.

Based on the Department of Justice's National Crime Victimization Survey, 2010-2014 (published in 2015) RAINN states, "every 98 seconds another American is assaulted" (RAINN 2018). Rapes most frequently occur in or near the victim's home, and most victims know the person or persons who attack them. This is not to say that stranger rape does not occur, only that it occurs less frequently than rapes perpetrated by someone known to the victim (For more on Stranger Rape, see Smith 2018). According to the World Health Organization, approximately "35 per cent of women worldwide have experienced either physical and/or sexual intimate partner violence or sexual violence by a non-partner at some point in their lives. However, some national studies show that up to 70 per cent of women have experienced physical and/or sexual violence from an intimate partner in their lifetime" (UN Women 2017).

Rape is underreported throughout the world. In the U.S., RAINN reports only fewer than one third of rape cases are reported, or 310 out of every 1,000 cases (RAINN, Criminal Justice 2018). In many parts of the world, marital rape is legal, and in general, women are expected to agree to sex with men. "Sixty-two percent of women and 48% of men agreed or partially agreed that a man has the right to sex even if a woman refuses" (Clinton Foundation and Bill & Melinda Gates Foundation 2015, 20).

Rape and sexual assault are perpetrated against men and boys, too. Nevertheless, such crimes are frequently never reported because the victims fear being stigmatized. This may happen in the military, for instance. It is especially problematic to report such cases in areas of the world where same-sex relationships are illegal, and thus reporting same-sex sexual violence puts the victim at risk of being arrested for participating in an illegal activity. In the United States, the FBI only changed the definition of rape to make it gender-neutral in 2013. However, state laws and definitions vary. The World Health Organization also has a gender-neutral definition of rape, but not all countries feel bound to honor this definition, and even in official studies, sexual violence against men and boys is less frequently studied. (For more on this topic, see Pellegrini 2018).

Individuals who identify as being LGBTQ are even more likely to experience sexual victimization than heterosexual individuals. The 2010 findings of the National Intimate Partner and Sexual Violence Survey revealed "some form of sexual violence were higher among lesbian women, gay men, and bisexual women and men compared to heterosexual women and men" (NISVS, n.d.).

23

For transgender individuals, sexual harassment, abuse, and assault face a greater risk of sexual harassment and violence. In a 2015 survey, nearly half of those who responded reported they were verbally harassed and/or sexually assaulted. Additionally, "nearly nine out of ten (86%) report[ed] being harassed, attacked, sexually assaulted, or mistreated in some other way by police," and they were "over five times more likely to be sexually assaulted by facility staff than the U.S. population in jails and prisons, and over nine times more likely to be sexually assaulted by other inmates." (James, et al. 2016, 15, 14).

It is impossible to cover sexual harassment and assault in a few pages. Accounts of sexual violence can be found in the earliest tales of humankind, and definitions of rape have changed throughout history. In this foreword, I have provided a few facts and figures. I am honored that the editors of this anthology, asked me to contribute some additional context to the volume.

Ninety-five writers and artists have spoken out courageously to break the silence. Though not all survivors of sexual harassment, abuse, and assault are able or willing to tell their stories, it is empowering for those who can, and it is enlightening for all to hear their stories.

Merril D. Smith is an independent scholar with a Ph.D. in American history. She is currently working on a book about sexual harassment. Merrill D. Smith is the author of An Encyclopedia of Rape.

Bearer of the Sky
Susan M. Conway

You spent your formative years having your ass handed to you or taken without consent. Your free will snatched from you and tossed aside along with your innocence and the capacity to ever be a child again.

And, through all of this-your precious face turned upward at the sky, tears streaming, heart screaming, you never once asked what was wrong with those that violated you; you wondered what was wrong with YOU. You sucked the shame and violence into your body like a dry sponge, and destroyed yourself instead.

Your immutable tenderness made for a devastating battleground, you got back up every time, swinging the weight of their blows over your shoulder so that you might never lose connection with THEIR LOVE. But their love hurt more and more the older and stronger your body grew.

The day you ran away, we were all with you, Sister. We coursed through your veins, our bare bloodied feet your thundering heart. Our collective, "My body is MY BODY. You don't get to hurt me anymore," woven into your flying hair as you ran, literally ran for your life. Our blood, your blood, Sister. Step for step, as alone and shameful as it felt pulling up your panties after having been beaten by your father, ass bared, menstrual blood trailing down your 13 year old legs- we were with you.

We were with you for every tear that spilled from your eyes, for every clean up on the bathroom floor, for every basement level desire to die. When you ran away, you swore to yourself that no one was ever going to hurt you again. So, you spent your life running into the arms of every lover and partner that your abusers had perfectly groomed you for. Atlas, you must let it crash down upon their heads sometimes.

Sky bearer, the burden of proof that your walking traumas despise to see, don't want living and breathing... We know it's beyond heavy but your testimony is needed. Other Sisters and Brothers are lost and spilling their own blood to be released from detail. You have a duty to heal, and to teach how to heal, to live a life so gorgeous it's hard to look at, a duty to serve and protect.

So, you MUST unsheathe that steel sword in your mouth. We beg of you to splay your guts, which are so very beautiful, to the sanctity of vulnerability. It has been 36 years and you have been so afraid of being touched again, that when kindness brushes your cheek with the back of her hand you still cringe. It is just that now, you have learned to leash and collar your fear, yanking it into socially palatable submission so as not to shift any of the weight you carry on your shoulders to anyone else.

You're still licking trauma's spit from your lips, Child.

I have faith, that one day you will emerge into the clearing that is the knowledge that although your abusers tasked you with the charge of holding up the sky, the entire Universe now revolves around you. Blessed Survivors, may you lean into the healing hard, may you step into the magnificence that you are. Bearer of stars, and moons, and mystery; sacred, sacred, sacred you are.

Little Girls
Jamie Lynn Martin

Little girls are not a novelty, they are
not a fetish.
They are not here to be stained by the
vulgarity belonging to your soul.
She does not want to be the object of
your lust,
nor does she need to understand the
depth of your desires.
Little girls are not bait for your assault.
They do bruise, and they break.
They love like all that is pure.
Little girls are bubble gum and daisies,
they dream in color, so vibrant you can
feel the warmth of her grace.
She is the breath of serenity, the bliss
of what we use to be.
Her scars will be sown into her shadow,
hiding in the corners of her smile.

Jamie Lynn Martin I Little Girls

Shrimp
Carla Schwartz

1.
We lived in a slab house,
shingled and dark.
We were renting back then.
Mommy painted us.

My blue umbrella was satin,
just the right size for my hands.
It was not really for rain,
more a parasol.

Powder blue umbrella in hand,
I started to cross the street to Gina's.

2.
I remember lying in the driveway,
Mommy waiting impatiently
for the ambulance
that took forever.
Then Mommy holding my hand.

Then the wheelchair,
the hospital,
the teeth shaken out of me,
being carried everywhere
for a week before I regained my balance,
and the get well cards
from nursery school.

Later, the visit to a doctor,
supposed to check my hearing,
who put his hand so deep

I had to bury the memory.

3.
I never liked shrimp growing up.
I thought it was because Mommy only cooked it frozen,
and it smelled like a frozen toilet.

Later, Mom said I used to love shrimp,
and that the day I was hit by the car,
I threw it up on the driveway,
and after that, I wouldn't eat shrimp again.

It was a long time before I knew
shrimp didn't have to stink.
I never told Mom about the bad doctor.
By the time I remembered,
I knew what it smelled like,
and I didn't know what
I remembered.

Go-Go Boots
S.L. Heaton

I remember my little white go-go boots sitting in the corner of my room.
And I remember how the light from the door cut through the dark so I could see those little white go-go boots sitting in the corner.
And I remember how he crept into my room and into my bed while I watched those little white go-go boots sitting in the corner.
And I remember how he said, "Lay like this,"
as I stared at those little white go-go boots sitting in the corner.
And I remember I laid so still, just like those little white go-go boots sitting in the corner.
A three year old doesn't remember a lot of things, but I will always remember those little white go-go boots sitting in the corner.

Behind Closed Doors
tara caribou

Quiet, little girl
Don't make a sound
Not a word
Mommy doesn't need to know
She doesn't love you like I do
I made you
You're mine
Keep real quiet
Let me see you
It pleases me to touch you
This is the way a Daddy loves his girl
Don't cry
No, don't cry
Don't you want me to love you?
Do what I tell you
Don't disobey
This feels good, it's right
This is how Daddy loves his little one
When I come to you next time
I want you ready
With no tears
If you don't obey I can't love you
Maybe next time Mommy leaves
You'll stay home with me instead?
Would you like that too?
I will show you just how much
A Daddy loves his baby girl
Don't cry
No, don't cry
Do you want my love?
Then don't ever cry again

Decades
A. Shea (Angie Waters)

Time has not erased the shiver
or the way my blood runs cold.
With the threat of probing
fingers,
I go back to four years old...
and the number of hands
in the decades since
that groped away
precious innocence
and replaced it with a rage
that has outgrown the silence.

A. Shea | Decades

The Innocence Is Haunting
Rachel Finch

We were timid girls,
that hadn't known it until
we weren't any more.
Taught how to keep our lips closed
and our legs open,
too small to know why until the first
hit,
too small to know how to stop the next.
We were a little nest of sparrows,
huddling to keep warm when the dark drew near,
too weak to sing, too fragile to fly.
She said to me, "how can you fear the wolf if you've never seen his
teeth bared?" and I thought back to the days I would
reach out my hand, with no knowledge of the bite.

Chores
Rachael Ikins

Mother taught me to hang father's shirts
by the folded collar tabs and cuffs on the line
near the tree where my swing once hung.
Boys running rampant, cowboys and Indians
"You pin pants from the bottoms, pockets turned inside out,"
a wooden clothespin clamped between her lips. Grandma
ironed later listening to the Victrola.

Hanging sheets was a two-woman job
even if one of the women was only 5 years old.
Big boys lurked under the apple tree,
swooped, scooped stolen tents or wizard capes
until Mother caught them. Whuppin' to pay, muddy
handprints on her clean wash.

Grandmother taught me how to iron men's shirts,
first the placket then the collar then cuffs,
sleeves and front halves then the back.
Between the clotheslines, boys holler war cries,
trousers saddled to their bikes.
Ironing board screeches
when Father sets it up under the cuckoo clock.

Arcana of laundry passed down woman to woman,
with piles of needlework, cross-stitched or creweled, baby gowns
and handkerchiefs, while boys chopped firewood, shingled a roof,
wilding the swamp; building forts, capturing dragons, chasing any
girls brave enough to follow, hidden beneath mud cheeks and grass
hair.
I wanted to be one of those boys.

Swamp song, peeper-loud,

Wind-swollen lilac.
From the fields, winter's manure fragrance
counterpoint.

At night, I rubbed Saturday sunburn
(because I lost my bonnet)
against smooth cool cotton, inhaled
that dried-on-the-line scent, home.

I turned 12. Uncle told me he'd teach me to milk the cows.
Bent me over a stool, crouched behind, grabbing my waist-
me scared of hooves and Bossy's swishing tail.
My forehead against her suede side, scent of her cud.
Rhythmic sounds; chewing, milk splashing bucket,
(he'd squirted me with it like I was a kitten when I was little,)

He calls me 'maturified.' My tears stripe her glossy black haunch.
He mutters "squeeze the teats."
I wonder why the cow doesn't move,
us banging into her belly, my fingers fisted
into her fur.

Wild boys,
Good girls.
Mother, Mommie?
How do you get blood
out of white sheets?

Secrets
Hanlie Robbertse

How do I break open this sealed tomb
of old shame and display it to the
sometimes hungry eyes of an easily
judging world while keeping myself
together? I've carried the secret of
your invasion of my innocence like
an old sack of bones that's turned
to dust and it's time to throw it
out and let it blow away in the wind.
Your violence didn't break me, but
the ensuing silence did. I was just a
child and did not understand why
it all was swept away and not talked
about. . . that's when I first learned
that even ones you love, cannot
be trusted for instead of protecting me,
I was left alone and I came to
understand: some things that are
supposed to be beautiful, were dressed
in red crimson hues of embarrassment.
It took me a long time to heal from
that moment when I lost so much of
myself, and some days I still fall
into pits of despair; but I'm slowly
finding the lost voice of that
confused, lonely little girl and
she is learning that speaking
truths that are sometimes hard,
brings healing and makes her strong.

Back Alley
Cynthia L Bryant

Back alley…
A misnomer, too benign
For such a vile deed
The place I was taken
To cover the heinous deeds of my father

The house was in disrepair,
rubble all around
the question of sanitary conditions
Answered simply by lifting eyes or nose

There, seated on well worn couches
Fidgety, frightened, forlorn women
I in my shame, hardly daring
To look up or glance around

Given a tranquilizer an hour before arrival
At the den of death
The corners of my vision softened
Ever so slightly

Mother sat by my side
Attempting small talk
A nervous ruthless culprit in crime
Determined to have her way

Strangers
Lead me down the darkened hallway
To a lighted room—
Given gas, almost immediately

Awakened into a nightmare:

Loud squealing, crashing sounds,
Brightly colored flashing lights
Assaulted my senses

As my molested body contracted to hold on
Sounds of a ruinous running remedy
Poured into some far away bucket
Outraged, my tortured mind screamed

I came to—two tampons crammed up
My young ravaged body
My fragile mind splintered beyond belief
Or caring

Father's sin washed away clean
Murderers paid in full
I was encouraged to leave, post haste

Home Safe
Lesléa Newman

Little Girl Blue,
What happened to you?
Who was it? Who?
And what did he do?

I was seven. Or eight.
Young enough to be still
unashamed of my body.

He was five. Or six.
Old enough to know a boy
could do what he wanted

to a girl who wasn't
the prettiest, the skinniest
the fairest in the land.

It was the children's hour,
that wild blue interlude
between supper and bedtime

when the moms were in their kitchens
washing off the dishes, and the dads
were in their dens gazing at TV.

All us kids were in the park
except for Mindy Finkelstein
whose father made her lie down

for an entire hour after she ate
so she could "digest." The rest
of us huddled close together

39

like a rack of pool balls
until Tommy Batista gave the signal
and we broke, scattering

across the green felt grass screeching
with joy, both the chasers and the chased.
We played Running Bases, TV Tag,

Ring-a-levio, Fox-and-Geese.
The sun went down. The breeze picked up.
Frogs croaked. Peepers peeped.

I was flying towards home
base which was Mrs. Barricolli's back yard.
We called her Mrs. Macaroni

which she knew and didn't mind.
All I had to do was tag the big oak tree
behind her two-car garage and I'd be safe.

I ran as if my life depended on it
and crashed into a boy
and tumbled to the ground.

He climbed on top of me.
He wasn't very heavy.
His head blocked out the last drop of sun.

Little Girl Blue,
Who was it? Who?

He didn't live on our block.
He was nobody's kid brother.
He didn't play by the rules.

He had grass stains on his dungarees,
blond Dennis the Menace hair
that whipped in the wind,

a small cut on his chin.
Big blue eyes. He was smaller
than me. But stronger.

Little Girl Blue,
What did he do?

He knew no one
else was around.
He knew I was cornered.

He knew he held me
in the grubby palm
of his dirt-streaked hand

which snaked its way
between my legs
where his curious fingers

furled and unfurled
curled and uncurled
like the sea anemone

I had once seen on a class trip
to the Bronx zoo.
That day I'd stood perfectly still

my hands and face pressed
against the cool glass,
hypnotized, mesmerized,

just as I was right now
as his fingers found that strange spot
inside me, a foreign country

I never knew existed,
a place that felt so good
I knew right away it was bad.

His fingers so gentle
against the thin seam of my pedal pushers
fluttering rippling tickling

Little Girl Blue
What did you do?

I didn't move
for a minute, an hour,
a lifetime, until something

streaked by—a firefly? a dog?
another kid? my big brother?
The boy took off and I crawled

to the tree. Home safe.
I waited until the lights
came on in the houses

all around me, and the moms
called their kids home
and the dads put out the trash.

Little Girl Blue
then what did you do?

I dragged my body home

like a bulky bag of groceries
I had trouble holding in my arms.

I never played in the park
again. I had homework, a headache,
a bellyache, I had to lie

down and digest
what had happened
in Mrs. Macaroni's back yard.

It took me fifty years
to realize how hurt
that little boy must have been.

Little Boy Blue,
What happened to you?
Who was it? Who?
And what did they do?

Not a Comma

Matthew D. Eayre

The hardest part always has been
that I enjoyed some of it
Being told that what happened was wrong and remembering my part
in what occurred has twisted my feelings toward myself for my whole
life.
Being taught, at an age too young to remember, that love and sex go
together, that physical pleasure comes from emotional contact and
vice versa, this has been a nearly impossible obstacle to overcome.
How should I straighten these tangles?
I've explored every angle and I've tried to discover what is important
and what is true
I was a child and I should have been protected
and my brother should have been protected before me
and my sister before him
and, I'm assuming,
my father should have been protected from what surely happened to
him
and the cycle stops with me, at least my part of this story is a period
and not a comma
My children are protected
and they know how to speak for themselves, they will not be silent
victims
as I was

the hardest part has always been
feeling culpable for what happened to me, and never have I been
able to break free of that feeling

I've paid for the words
it wasn't my fault, no matter how I processed the way it felt
I was unable to give informed consent for what happened to my
body.

I've paid for the words
I should have been protected and the failure of my mother can be
forgiven but never excused
I deserved better

I've paid for the words
and even if I never tell the whole story
I'm not afraid anymore

Don't say a word
Madame K Poetess

Shhh. . .
Don't say a word,
It is our little secret;
Was the last thing I heard

He was far too strong for me.
As a young girl
I was much too weak;
I couldn't scream,
I couldn't speak.
I cried in silence
No matter the pain, I felt
Or how much it hurt,
All I could think was;
Shhh. . .
Don't say a word.

Taking the innocence
Of, what was, already
a broken little girl,
I had seen
enough violence
But then
along came he,
An animal, A predator
He took away, from me
more than my innocence,
He took away my voice.
I had lost all hope;
No longer could I trust
The Adults of this world.

He wasn't the first,
It had happened before.
But how was I to know
He wouldn't be the last,
There would be more
predators to come;
There was no one
to protect me
once night came
& by morning
I'd be left
feeling ashamed.
Now, as an adult
I know that I was
not the one at fault.
But them,
Who stole the innocence
of a child,
Those animals
Are the ones to blame.

& these memories arise
by that one little phrase;
Shhh ...
This is our little secret,
Don't say a word.

Ripping the tape
Jesica Nodarse

I cannot quietly fade into the background I will not
even contemplate it
My voice is precious
My lungs would become rusty if I contained all this
rage
This rage that I inherited
The one my mama had to bare
The same her mother gifted her
On the eve of her ninth birthday, when her voice
failed her

**Jesica Nodarse |
Ripping the tape**

Magical Thinking
Christine E. Ray

I hide myself behind the hanging coats
praying to a god I already no longer believe in
to turn me chameleon
like the ones I read about
in fourth grade
plead with the universe
make my pale skin and dark hair
blend in with the parkas
make my left arm plaid
my cheek blue polka dots
to please make the piled winter boots and sneakers
provide camouflage for corduroyed legs
stockinged feet
cold and wet from melting snow
Please, I beg whatever powers might listen
let his eyes pass over me unseen
let me be invisible to those unblinking eyes
that made me feel so dirty
so repulsive
so naked
just this once

Safety at Age Eleven
Wilda W. Morris

Grandmother would have kept me
safe had she known her beloved nephew
visiting from Kansas would trap me
on the basement stair and touch me
in the wrong places. I kept her safe
from heartbreak by not telling.

And Mother would have kept me safe
had she suspected. She'd warned me
about strangers, told me where to kick
if I needed to get away, but she was at work
and had too many worries already
so I kept her safe, too.

I didn't go to the basement again
until he was back on the west-bound train.
And until now, I never told anyone.

Driven Thru
Deirdre Fagan

When you are 13 and poor,
even Taco Bell has an allure.

The Monte Carlo that held us
had a sheepskin bench seat.

Its soft cover like a fitted sheet
curving its corners like a cloud.

Seatbelts weren't worn in 1983;
no need for slits to let safety peer in.

"Come closer and you can steer," you said.

Nearly half my current size, no breasts,
thighs the width of my current calves --

I leaned full-bodied into the drive
eyes on the road, mouth watering,
drive-thru beckoning.

(What is there to taking a young girl?)

*"Driven Thru," originally appeared in New Verse News and may be
viewed here:
https://newversenews.blogspot.com/2018/01/driven-thru.html*

Thirteen
Aubrey Dunn

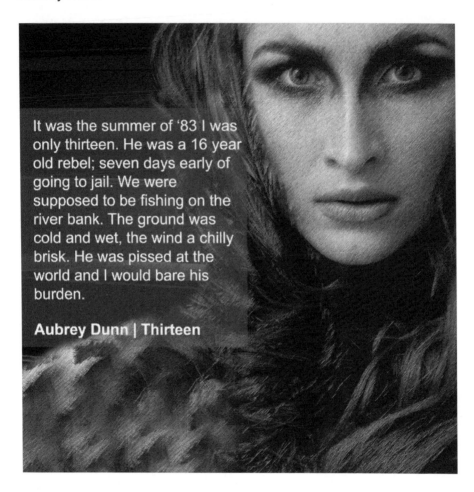

It was the summer of '83 I was only thirteen. He was a 16 year old rebel; seven days early of going to jail. We were supposed to be fishing on the river bank. The ground was cold and wet, the wind a chilly brisk. He was pissed at the world and I would bare his burden.

Aubrey Dunn | Thirteen

Lock Her Up
Cynthia Bryant

Somewhere
to a nonplussed audience
 of her parents
a molested daughter
blurts out the secret
about her lately pouting tummy
how it came to pass

Somewhere
a mother screams
unintelligible sounds rise
to blot out offending words
that present too hard a choice
Calls the police
on her canary-yellow kitchen phone

Somewhere
the fury of a father
shocks high-color to face
as he pummels daughter
in attempts to exorcise
the madness
that threatens exposure

Somewhere
nosey neighbors open front doors
stand in groups in their yards
make up minds by committee
about what sort of folks
and who's at fault
when laundry is aired

Somewhere
small town police arrive
lights flashing
as parents point to daughter
an undone puzzle on the floor
police gather the pieces
pile her into the back of a squad car

Somewhere
an unheard daughter
serving one-month solitary in Juvenile Hall
revisits over and over
the last few moments at home
  outnumbered
     incorrigible

Sleepover
Deirdre Fagan

a plaid pullout worn down down down
springs poking deep my tiny back
a blanket slowly uplifted

cool air shocking warm slim thin thighs
stomachpelvisclenched muscles tight
large hands and cotton underwear

the panties pulled quietly aside
lips first felt hot wet pointed tongue
thick fingers slowly entered then

i tried to control my breathing
and pretend i was still sleeping
in the next room your wife asleep

the next morning i dare not say
mother sent me over to stay
fourteen – first sleepover away

dark intentions
Linda M. Crate

"i bet you don't remember me," you smirked with that devil may cry
grin; and i froze like a doe in the headlights, unable to move—i
remember being little more than a girl and you were my boyfriend
and your sister wasn't watching us, of how powerless and angry you
made me feel when you kissed my lips thrice when i told you no all
three times; of how terrified i was when you tried to force yourself on
me—but in a rush of adrenaline somehow i was able to keep hold of
my flowers, my innocence was shattered though; i realized that the
big bad wolf's of little red riding hood weren't strangers but rather
people you thought you knew—there was no turning back to that girl i
once was, and every time i hear the compliment, "you have a pretty
smile" i hear your voice saying the same thing; and i am haunted by
it—such a nice thing to have someone say to me, and yet i cannot
embrace it as i should because i am reminded of you and your dark
intentions.

When I say I Am Ticklish I Mean I Am Scared of Men
Joey Gould

I don't mean fathers holding their children five feet closer
to the sun: nearer that small warm. Men are capable.
A man once held me when I shook tears

like a wet dog. A man once made me cry for more,
searching where he could touch without repel. He had
my consent but my body laughed sarcastically.

It remembers what my mouth doesn't
& collapses, armadillo-ing, or rather turtling away.
If you are a very good man I should kiss you

but my thighs are scared. Remember that night
when the concert emptied & he walked
alone? I held my car key like a dull knife.

Because men are capable of—
[inaudible dialogue]

don't make us say it. Any of us.

& I know you, I *know* you. I knew him, too
& he could ice skate backwards, he had hockey hair,
he had jewels for eyes & smelled like rain—

what does it matter? How can I take
anyone's recommendation over my own skin?
Skin which has kept my blood its whole life,

which bruised against the schoolyard pavement
& remembers. It holds what my mouth would spit.
What it had to. Sometimes it glows red for no reason,

I tell myself: for no reason.

"Someone asked if I am concerned
that others will assume I am the
speaker of my poems, as if I am
ashamed. I am the speaker. You are
the speaker.
This anthology is important to all of
us."

Amanda Forrester

My Body Remembers
Christine E. Ray

my body remembers
what my mind tries to forget
why don't you drive?
innocent question asked
unexpectedly serves as key
to the locked door of memory
transported back in time
teenager without a license
forced to accept a ride
I did not want

my body remembers
idling in the driveway
praying someone else is home
tinny voice of the Red Socks announcer
droning out the play by play
on the cheap AM radio
the smell of Tijuana Smalls
mixed with his cologne
(a scent that still makes me ill)
mingles with the odor
of my anxiety
I sit as far away from him
as the small sedan will allow
curl myself defensively
around my exposed left side
swallowing down the panic
harsh as gravel
in my throat
will he let me get out
without incident
or will he cut me with words

trying to trigger my self-loathing
shame?
will he invent an excuse
to touch me with those sweaty hands
marking me unclean
leaving his fingerprints scorched
on my skin?

I am older now
14 maybe 15
stronger
angrier
but I have been asked
not to make a scene
be grateful for this favor
to smile and say thank you
I will play nice if he does
I think to myself
the words as sharp as
shark teeth in my head

my body remembers
how desperately I long
to be anywhere but here
in this locked metal cage
with my tormentor
my abuser

my body remembers

The Morning After
S.L. Heaton

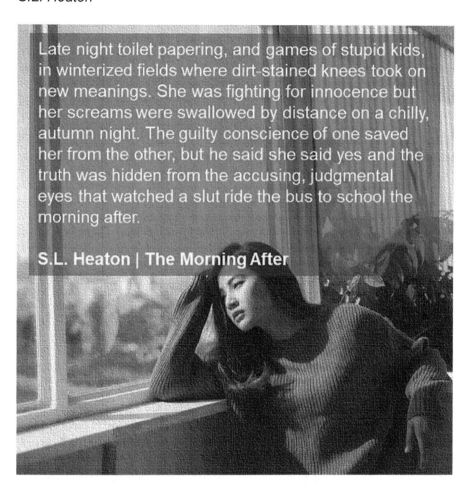

Late night toilet papering, and games of stupid kids, in winterized fields where dirt-stained knees took on new meanings. She was fighting for innocence but her screams were swallowed by distance on a chilly, autumn night. The guilty conscience of one saved her from the other, but he said she said yes and the truth was hidden from the accusing, judgmental eyes that watched a slut ride the bus to school the morning after.

S.L. Heaton | The Morning After

Clothed
Michelle Bradway

Do you know the feeling when you press your gloved fingers together on a cold winter morning? You can still feel the pressure of the oval pads against one another despite the wool. In the silence that accompanies the roaring wind you can hear your pulse beat between your hands. And you remember what it feels like to touch your palms together when they are bare. So even through the thick static of your gloves blocks the flesh you know the sensation. You know it. You feel it.

Just the same, when you pushed yourself against the entrance of my body, I felt it. I knew it. It didn't matter that you were wearing those shorts. For a long time I thought it did. Thought it made it untrue. That it didn't count. Even though I said no and tried to get away, held down by the weight of your arms and legs, I believed your gym shorts made you innocent, clean.

We were fifteen and clothed, but I never felt more naked, dirty.

As I got older I met some remarkable women. I was sure they had made it through childhood unscathed. The only way to appear worthy of their friendship was to continue telling myself that your shorts separated me from the 1 in 3. I was part of the two. The two that's not even true.

See, there really aren't two, that's what I came to find. Because those remarkable women, they also had one of you. You's who made them believe for one reason or another that what had happened was clean and different and fine. Just fine. Well we started talking and compared scars and shared rage.

And would you guess what we found?

It's not innocent, clean, different or untrue. And it's certainly not fine. No. It's really not fine. What I want to say is…
What I want to march down the streets with my sisters and scream is…

"Don't expect me to stand cold in the snow pretending I don't know what my own flesh feels like anymore."

Fifteen
Dawn D
*

Walking through an empty alley
In the center of the city,
Baggy jeans, funky purple tee,
Coloured hair, finally happy.
*

Lost in a pop-song, lip-syncing
Busy thoughts fill my head, rushing;
I walk past a lone man leaning
On a wooden door, doing my thing
*

Suddenly, I hear a faint sound
Through my music, it's almost drowned
I free an ear and look around
The man is right there, as if wound
*

Ready to jump me, in my face
He pushes me against the wall
I'm struggling, I have no space
I start to panic, want to bawl
But no sound escapes, not a trace
Not a single peep, none at all
*

He lifts my crop top
Fondles me
I ask him to stop
Leave me be
"We'll just have fun
It's Okay"
"This is NOT fun
I want away"
*

But still he pushes me

Against the concrete wall
I think that's when my soul
Detached from my body
*

He reeks of alcohol,
He looks in his thirties
That's more than twice my age
Don't want to see his face
I can feel his penis
Pressing against my thigh
How on earth did my pants
Get to be down my thighs?
His hand is splitting me
Don't want his finger there
He pushes in. It hurts
Now he's shoving me down
I'm sitting on the ground
He forces my mouth open
Thrusts his erection in
I'm gagging, I'm frozen
I watch, numb, from above
Wondering what comes next
Will he penetrate me?
Maybe even kill me?
I'm sitting, tears gushing
In long streams on my cheeks
I'm powerless, lost.
*

A young man comes running,
Barely out of his teens
But brave beyond his years,
Throws a hard punch at him
My assaillant flees the scene
My savior helps me get up
Brings down my tee, pulls back my jeans

"You are safe now" and he hugs me
Until, slowly, I get calmer,
Am able to stand by myself
He then walks me to the station
Stays with me until I feel safe
Sitting in the bus, going home
*

Safe...
Will I ever feel safe again?
I wonder, sobbing in the rain
Of the shower. Yet I can't seem
To be safe, even in my dreams
I feel dirty, but I must feign
Normalcy, don't want to cause pain
To my parents. I want to scream
But I can't speak, fear the extreme
Moves they would take to protect me
When all I want is to be free
To live my life, not to concede
Power to this man and his deed
Control is the last thing I need
*

Yesterday morning,
In broad daylight
I was raped.
I'm not even fifteen.

Sixteen
Nikita Goel

He said
He loved me
For the red tint on my cheeks
Tender smile on my face
Deep dark eyes
For whom I was
I believed him.
He said
He wanted me
Staring at my bosom
I did not know
What he meant.
Tender was my age
I turned 16
He took me somewhere
A place where nobody came
I was scared.
I wanted to cry
I could not scream
He did not let me.
Like a savage
He tore me
And feasted
On my body
I shiver
When I think
Of that day
My body
Bled for a day
I could not walk
I did not talk
I felt undressed

Every time
I felt ashamed
Of what he did to me
I cursed myself
For trusting him.

"Being a part of this means so much to me because it gives a voice to someone that no longer has theirs. Their voice was stolen, and I will scream to the top of my lungs to give it back."

Jamie Lynn Martin

1992
Stephanie Bennett-Henry

I wonder if your football jersey still smells like arms pinned down, muffled screams, echoes of no that sounded like yes to you, and I wonder how many other hands ripped at that varsity jacket, hoping to god, they were strong enough to keep their knees together, just before you took what could never be returned. I wonder if you swallowed the screams like a championship title with that filthy grin on your face, or if your hands still hold teethmarks of no and breath that tasted desperation too heavy to move. I still pray you have choked to death on each unheard no by now, but I know you are alive and well, while I live each day dying inside. I wonder if 1992 still calls you a hero.

Some Other Girl
Lola White

In Bombay, India, on August 14, 2002, a 17-year-old-girl was raped on a crowded train while commuters watched and did nothing. The suspect was arrested immediately after the assault, and faces a minimum of ten years in jail, if convicted. The girl was sent to a hospital where her waist-length hair was shaved because of lice.

I was not the girl on the train,
that must have been some other girl.
That girl had long, black hair.
I have no hair. She had a voice.
I have none. I was not that girl.

That girl screamed and sobbed.
The people shouted, but did
not help her. I know,
I was watching, silent as a bird,
from a perch above the crowd.

That was another girl,
with long hair and a voice.
That is why I write these words.
And if I could speak,
what would I say?

I was not the girl in the train,
I don't want to think about her.
I only want to think of the peacocks in my village,
their noble bearing, their regal crowns,
their sweeping, iridescent trains.

The peacocks in my village were ravishing
in their breastplates of lapis lazuli,
their fans of turquoise, teal, and gold.

Their piercing screams.
Whether my eyes are open or closed,
I see only the peacocks' beauty,
hear only their screams.

"A single voice has the power to awaken the many. It takes great courage to face our buried pain. By speaking our truth, we can help others speak their truth too. Together, we will not be silenced anymore."

Michèle Duquet

Rain
Mary Hansen

You weren't my first date, but you were the one I always wanted.
I thought we would play goofy golf, or go bowling, maybe take in a film.
But you had a better idea.

Let's go for a drive in the rain, you said.
I remember sitting in your truck as you drove to the outskirts of town.
The soft rain steadily became more insistent as you drove.

After a while, you parked your truck and pulled me closer.
I was willing, compliant, eager to be close. The rain drummed steadily on the truck.

When you wanted more than a kiss, I said no.
You suddenly became nasty and accusing, calling me names.
You pulled a revolver out of your glove compartment.
You pointed it at me and demanded.

I remember the rain on the windows and lightning in the distance.
I remember being strangely unafraid of the weapon.
I remember the look on your face.

It was over in moments, but the memory of shame lingers yet.
Later I would try to wash it from my mind and body.
That night I pretended to enjoy the scenery after the rain.

Now when it rains, I always shiver, wondering who is lurking out of sight.
I wonder if I will be alright when the rain stops.
I wonder if I curl up and try, will I be able to stay dry?

Old Man Hands
Rachel Woolf

*"Every wound ever suffered remains within a tree, but while they may
not heal, most trees do get closure."**

The last time I saw the
old man's
dirty hands
he was dead
in the wooden
open casket–
I didn't mean to see him.

Old man
liver spots
gnarled hands
could do no harm
I was relieved.
She was so happy;
almost gave me a high-five.

They caught him in the
nursing home:
dirty old man,
grabbing nurses
while he still could,
no remorse–
he did it all of his life.

Dirty hands,
old man
grabbing daughters
and granddaughters,
grabbing me.

How many wounds,
how many scars did he carve?

The last time, I remember:
the old man limping,
the baseball game,
the parking lot;
I walked beside him.
"You are my friend",
he said, and then he grabbed me.

I brushed him off.
I didn't know
it was not the only time.
I don't remember
the other times,
but my body does—
you cannot stand behind me.

Until the end,
no one talked about it—
just the whispers.
"Lock the door" she told me.
"I can't be touched like that",
she said, no explanation.
Anger buried deep inside.

When it came out—
"We didn't know,"
said his sons.
They scolded him sternly,
demented old man.
That was all,
as if it never happened.

Rough old man
He used his hands
To build stone walls,
And carve wood toys
And to destroy.
I have grown over
The scarring wounds inside me.

*Michael Snyder, Woods Whys: How Do Trees Heal Wounds on
Trunks and Branches? January 19, 2016

Jesus Saves
Rachel Kobin

In my forties, when the memory of the event surfaced, I used to joke with my friends about what happened to me when I thought I was safely sleeping in my all-women's dorm: I woke up to find a boy lying on top of me. I had met him at the computer center earlier that night. Before I had time to understand what he was trying to do, he said something about Jesus and left. How funny that a young Jewish woman would be saved by Jesus. Ha.

I locked the door and went right back to sleep, but in the days that followed, I descended into what I now know was full-blown mania. My parents drove down and retrieved me from the emergency room. I didn't tell them what had happened because I had disassociated so effectively that I didn't remember for another twenty years. I spent the rest of that school year recovering from the depression that followed the mania.

As I read the #metoo posts and tweets, I thought of myself as lucky because what happened to me wasn't nearly as bad as what has happened, and continues to happen, to so many women. Inured to our rape culture—like so many of us have been—I diminished the impact of my own experience. Then I found myself typing #metoo. He broke into my room. I woke up to the weight of a man's body on top of me. I saw a face I knew. As the moisture of his breath hit my face, he said these exact words: "This isn't what Jesus would have done."

Handlebar
Robin Anna Smith

borrowing a car   we take Amtrak to the suburbs

Windows down on the highway in your mom's Impala. We're making our way down I-90, toward Indiana. It's offensively hot, but we don't mind. Happy to be getting out of the city for a few days. "Don't Stop Believin'" blares from the radio and we're belting it out.

I'm riding shotgun and from the corner of my eye, I notice a motorcycle. Absorbed in song, I don't pay much attention. It creeps back up again and then falls back. Still singing, I make note of the biker's face. A few moments later, the same guy is coming up on the driver's side.

Suddenly you shout "Oh my God!" and swerve. He's flicking his tongue at us like Gene Simmons. His pants are unzipped and he's beating off, balls flapping in the wind. We scream, roll up the windows, and try to pull away. He speeds up next to us, never slowing down the activity of his hand.

Miles pass, as we try to think of other deterrents, none of which would work. We are panicking. *Should we get off at the next exit? What if he follows us? We should throw something at him. But what if he crashes and dies? Will we go to jail?*

He abruptly veers away onto an exit ramp, smiling and nodding at us with satisfaction. Dick in hand—still going...

Chicago 'L' train   stars follow me home from the platform

originally published in Rhythm & Bones, Issue Two, October 2018

Bruise
Sally Zakariya

They said he might be gay but I knew better –
didn't he pick my little flower that summer
there on the upper bunk in the room he shared
with his brother, knocking my knee so hard
against the wall he built a bruise.

I sailed to Europe the next day treasuring
that bruise, touching it for the warm
memory it made.

We were three college girls adventuring
in a beat-out Mercedes, but by the time
we got to Italy the bruise was fading.

One night a young Italian man, dark
and slightly dangerous, took me to a field
outside of town, then took what he expected –
quid pro quo for my first ride on a Vespa
black as his greasy curls.

In a later age they'd call it date rape.
Back then some called it free love, but
love that night had nothing to do with it –
just a new intimate but invisible bruise.

it didn't, it doesn't, it won't
Linda M. Crate

vulnerable, depressed
i was looking to take a walk
to clear my head;
you insisted it was dark instead
so i agreed to talk to you
in your room
where you apparently wanted
netflix and chill
straining to see a movie i didn't even like
to keep from kissing you,
you decided it would be a good idea
to force my hand down
your pants;
i recoiled as if i had touched a snake
and you bit in with the fangs of your anger
like you had any right to be upset—
you only calmed the ocean
of your fury
when i expressed that one of my exes
tried to rape me
as if it would otherwise be wrong for me to reject
your advances
like being nice to me
gave you some right to me or my body
it didn't, it doesn't, and it won't.

Finally
Anonymous Was a Woman

I finally said no
I finally tried to stop you
To push you away
But you overpowered me
Physically
And you held me in place

With a hand on my throat
And arm on my chest
The other gripping my hair and
The back of my neck
You held me in place
You said "I'm not done"
I was frozen
Except for the vomit on my tongue

But you didn't kiss me
You just needed to cum
And when you finally let go
I was shattered and numb

You left, like it was any other day
And I suppose it was, in a way
It wasn't the first time
You'd taken me that way
But it was the last

I won't keep your silence anymore

The Eddies
Holly Rene Hunter

He smiled sweetly and said he was lonely,
let's go for a ride down by the dunes.
Retracting the top of his new convertible
we sped along freeways and deserted back roads
while the radio blared Louie Louie.
I remember the sea wall where we drank straight
from the bottle until the swallow no longer burned.
The moon and the stars sunk behind his shoulder
and my stifled cries seemed to drown in the sea.
While my father slept I scrubbed my bruises
watched pools of red eddy at the drain.
You think I'm no body to use as you please
but I'm not just somebody who's all alone.

Slap
Betty Albright

He said he liked
the way I walked,
sang Dean Martin
with his motorcycle cocked
till I went with him
to Sehome Hill
and he stopped being Dean
and the meadow grew thorns
as he twisted my slap
grinding into the shock
knowing I'd never tell,
for back then
women blamed themselves

Companion
Megha Sood

Loneliness sits at the edge of my bed.
His eyes gazing from emptiness to nothing.
The room is white and there is not an iota of aberration
everything is picture perfect.
You make a sound, a sliver of noise
filtering from the jammed cracked window
and it will alter the balance of this pristine
picture perfect room
it will claw its way into the loneliness
and give it a companion
my loneliness is pitch perfect
it doesn't need a companion
the screams and scratches are best heard
in the vacuum
where nothing can travel
and it enjoys the soliloquy
the spotlight
it deserves
it echoes in the dark and the
presence can be felt in the
a dark circle of my eyes
the dark bird circles around the moon
before getting sucked in
the faintest of the voices can
add to the cacophony in my head
as my thoughts need
the utter pin drop silence
as I'm dressed in my favorite birthday dress
and I need all the attention
your slithering fingers need
as they crawl under my dress
my loneliness needs no companion

it has the company of the yellow moon
I gulped as I screamed
under my *muted* breath.

"My mother was in her 60's before she ever told anyone about the abuse she had suffered starting at six years of age. Silence only reperpetuates the problem. Objectification, exploitation and abuse of women is more than a common experience - it is an epidemic that needs to be addressed. Telling our stories opens the door to honest dialogue. As a society, we should hold a higher vision for generations."

V.J. Knutson

As if That Would Be Love

Carrie Weis

You ask to sit, as you pull the passenger door open
my answer swirling above your head
and into the wind, as you take a seat

Reluctantly, I climb in
my car now smaller than I knew it to be
You unzip your pants
pulling out a dark, flaccid penis
my words now without wings

You grab my hand
with the one, not full of your skin
and beg me to touch it
as if that would be love

Like countless times before
Dawn D

Today,
I got to realise what rape is.
Rape is the friend who's coming over,
Like countless times before.
Who, once you're finished with work,
Kisses you,
Like countless times before.
And you melt,
Like countless times before.
But then he starts to fondle you,
Like countless times before.
And you don't really want to,
Unlike countless times before.
But your body reacts exactly
Like countless times before,
So he doesn't really see the difference
With those times before.
You walk him to the door
Like countless times before
And he grabs you by the waist
Like countless times before.
You try to say NO,
But you're half laughing,
Because you don't want to hurt his feelings
Because that's what you've been told is important
Other people's feelings.
And when he slips his hand down your pants
Like countless times before,
You give up, your mind shuts down,
Like countless times before.
All those times when you were abused before
When you had to dissociate,

Let your body carry the weight
But preserve your mind,
Preserve the promise of life,
Of a better future,
Of the life you can live,
The lives you've born into this world,
Who need you still.
And so you let him do it,
Like countless times before
And you do what he asks
Like countless times before.
And yes, your body felt pleasure
Like countless times before
But your soul died a little more
Like countless times before.
Once again, you were just
A receptacle
Where someone empties his balls
And leaves you feeling dirty,
Like countless times before.
*

And it's hard to accept,
Because you let it happen,
So it's a bit your fault, isn't it?
Just like that time before
When you met your ex and thought
"Yes, it's true I teased him tonight.
Now I've got to see it through
And accept the consequences."
*

And it's hard to accept,
Because he is your friend
And you know he wouldn't have wanted it
If only he had known
The secret too many men don't understand

Or prefer to ignore:
If she's not saying yes
Check with her.
Chances are,
She really means no.
*
And it's hard to accept,
Because a month later,
When you think about it
You can still feel
In your throat,
The taste of his sperm
Choking you.

The Temple of Doom
Tiffany K Elliott

Dim blue flickers,
the voices and soundtrack
disorganize, their transference
to bootleg making Harrison Ford bumble
his lines, as your lips press
and part. The flicker staccatos your
lightly-stubbled chin, and as your hand
reaches down, I block with quaking fingers.
I block your advance, zipper pulled,
and you look down, down where soft
blackness pokes between the bars of my fingers,
insufficient barrier, as the TV
glows the night blue. It was
night that time, too, the night
I can't remember,
except for lying on my back,
cockroach-exposed,
his face blurred through tears, the
1970s motley-orange fashion spread
slick underneath. I couldn't stop
Darius—yes, I'll say his name
now, though I couldn't say anything for
years, afraid no one would believe
the girl who couldn't remember. You pull
the zipper down, slowly, ghoul
smile, like drawing out
my unwillingness turns you on. And I say no,
I pull away, but
as Indiana Jones whips
out his weapon on screen and you reach to yours,
I am afraid. I remember the old man on the Greyhound
when I was fifteen, nice

-seeming, and for hours we talked
about books and poetry
until the cabin filled
with snores and magazines and meaningless
murmuring. And then his hand
on my rounded thigh, high up
on my thigh. In Tucson
I hid, peeked through
the hinged restroom doorway for twenty
minutes until he walked away
defeated. And as you press on me
and reach down to
the prize, and as the golden temple
on screen crumbles, you pull
the metallic zipper with a wolfish
glare, pull it up, and you say
I am lucky
because you could have
done it if you really wanted to.
I breathe again.
How well I know that is true.

My Silence Burned
AmyKCM

It had been an extremely long night. We just finished up the third call in a row with no sleep. I sat in the dimly lit office, finished writing up the last run sheet and wearily pushed back my chair, hoping to catch a few quick winks before the alarm went off again.

I hadn't even heard him come in. Standing silently in the shadows of the office, was my shift Captain. Before I had a chance to consider anything, I was flung against the hard, cinder-block wall. I didn't even get the sound of my hard exhale, after hitting the wall, before his hand was over my gaping mouth. I tried to struggle, but couldn't move as the force of his body pressed against mine. His knee began a merciless prying and trying to spread my legs apart as I urgently tried to resist. His free hand began ravaging my breasts, groping, clawing and grabbing in his frantic attack.

He spoke few words between guttural groans. "Yes!" "Damn!" "I've always wanted this." "You feel amazing."
I desperately tried to speak only one. "No!"

I'm not sure what the loud noise was out in the engine bay, but it made him stop. He looked from the closed door and back at me wide eyed. Tears streamed down my face as he looked back at the door and released the pressure of his body on mine. He turned as if to leave, then quickly turned back to me, put his face close to mine and whispered through gritted teeth, "This NEVER happened!" A quick, hard kiss to my mouth and he was out the door. I stood there dumbfounded. I couldn't move. I couldn't breathe. I had no idea what to do next. I suddenly reached over and locked the office door and collapsed into a tiny quivering ball on the floor, behind the door, for the remainder of the night.

I was now, unexpectedly, the one in need of rescue.

Epilogue:

I believed no one would believe me, so I said nothing. He was a well-respected Captain. His wife was the station Secretary. I had already battled through the narrow minded belief held by many that I shouldn't be working in this profession anyway. This would only cement the warped views of all those I had fought against. I'd be just another whining woman that tried to do what men should be doing. And I was terrified.

I avoided shifts with him, best I could, after that. I tried to hide my fear and trepidation, but it seemed like others knew something was wrong. He became quite gruff and nasty with me. I couldn't seem to do anything right when he was around. I could hear him talking poorly of me with the other men and then laughing about it. I was still scared.

One night, another Captain in the Department pulled me aside to talk. I could tell he was nervous. I thought he might know. Maybe he was going to help me? Maybe he was going to protect me? He hemmed and hawed and finally blurted it out. He wanted to warn me to watch my back when it came to the Captain who had attacked me. He seemed to have it out for me and my other Captain just thought I should know so I could be careful. I wasn't even given a chance to comment. He turned and walked away, leaving me there completely numb, dumbstruck and feeling victimized all over again.

The Mandarin Fruit Seller
Marilyn Rea Beyer

Who was I but an unimportant girl?
He was a man of high office in a fine suit;
I pleased him with sweet rice and apricots.
He covered me with silvery words until my eyes closed
                 and I was lost in sighs.
I raised my eyes to him and he was gone.

You came later with pain and furrowed brow.
You cried because you knew not how to speak.
I wept because I could not find the words.

I carried you for two days.
The rough road broke my sandals, the sun burned my lips.
At last I found the yellow house filled with cribs
                 filled with other unimportant girls
Where the kind woman took you from my frightened arms.

I wonder - if you saw me at the fruit stand, would you know my eyes?

Finding Jay
Carla Schwartz

The first time I Google Jay, I fail.
Next, I try phone lookup, Massachusetts. Bingo.
Several towns listed, including my own.

I might have stood behind him at the market.
I might have collected his concert ticket.
So why today, was I thinking of Jay?
I walk away from the computer.

When I return, I Google his name + his town.
I land on an obituary — dead 3 months. *Suddenly,*
Christmas Eve. It could have been drugs.
Could have been suicide. Could have been his heart.
I know it's him.

Several loving memorials mention his company.
The company Jay, my boss, ran thirty years ago.
He was bossy. He had a mucousy voice.
A river of anger, driven by money,
by drugs, by girls.

He shared. He demanded.
I was a girl.
A *Girl Friday* — reception.

I still remember the yeasty smell.
The girth of his penis, as wide as a bouquet of stems.
His hand on my head, as if to press a button.
The sickly sweet between my teeth.

She's Just an Elevator
Melissa Fadul

temporary transport
      away from the marriage
of suits and lies to a lobby in a motor inn.

Some guy pays to enter.
      The owner ignores her face
that doesn't match her picture ID.

He winks & hands the nameless a key
      to a cabin whose floors are soaked
in bootprints of other Johns.

Bugs move between plaster & wallpaper,
      same as her daughter reading Braille—
fingers swimming across the page's pool

like a typewriter carriage before its ding
      sings, *you got a second? Get out of this now.*
Cold hands jolt her back,

bend and hoist her over a table
      garnished in fake roses caked in dust.
Pressing her face into the wood over&over,

he's in a hurry to get back to work
      she's the up and down button
that will make him come faster.

She tries to ignore her worn and sore shaft
      with dreams of her daughter
before cancer took her vision.

This helps her open
        for seconds then slowly seals herself
with a stranger inside.

"My experience of sexism has been layered in
silence. Don't make a fuss, don't complain, don't
whine. Don't advocate for your rights, it's too
aggressive. Don't call that person out, it's too
uncomfortable. The #MeToo movement was born
out of a collective rejection of silence: it
highlighted how horrifically damaging silence can
be. This anthology is a voice for the hurt and
frustrations that years of silence have built up—
and can hopefully begin to make some noise."

Rebecca Cairnes

Whiskey and Scotch
Beth Couch

I am always the villain in this story.

Boundaries of more than clothes
and skin and muscle and bone
separate me from him.
An insurmountable distance
measured out
not
in coffee spoons
but
in wives,
in husbands,
in children.

It would not be worth it after all
to hear him say,
That is not what I meant at all;
that is not it at all.

He turns, closing the door as he leaves.

Beneath the text messages,
the emails,
the meetings,
and the coffee,
I drown.

***

I told you
I am always the villain in this story,
so call me a prophet, a whore, a slut,

a homewrecker—
Elijah and Jezebel both.

I went willingly to you.
That is the Narrative,
is it not?
The Narrative to fill
the black emptiness.

A hysterical woman
preying on a good,
upstanding
husband and father;
not the other way around—
surely.

I am your downfall
and your nakedness
and your shame.
I am the girl who makes boys sin,
the one you called your dearest friend
as you whispered
"sweet dreams"
night
after night
after night
after night
after night
after night.

And I am here,
lost in the blackness of a memory
lost to the glasses long empty
of the whiskey and the scotch
that you poured.

I am always the villain in this story.
I am the girl who makes boys sin.

I dared disturb the universe,
I squeezed it into a ball,
but
I should have worn my trousers rolled
and let my hair thin.
That is not what I meant at all.

I should have drowned in my own silence.

If I could take back those nights, would I?
If I could take back those words, would I?
And was it worth it after all?

I don't know.

I don't think it was.

I don't think it was.

I don't think it was.

At the Blue Swallow by the Sea Motel
Marilyn Rea Beyer

You can get a room by the hour,
But she stayed the whole week.
Nothing here seemed real to her, not even the name of the town.
Unalaska.
She'd come on her own with just her little valise
And more baggage than anyone her age should carry.
Just a little rest she told herself, that's what was wanted here.

She made to fluff the pillow.
It was heavier than she expected.
Every fear and fault of 23 years half afloat in a broken boat in her
midnight mind.
Flotsam and jetsam.
Some she threw overboard, some just refused to sink.
Tired she was, yet open-eyed, blinking between the neon and the
moon.
Scared of the dark, but afraid of the sunrise.

The old phone jumped, a jagged ring she didn't hear
Through the noise gnawing in her head.
A knock on the door brought her to. The motel man smelling of bed
saying,
"There's a guy here for you. Says it's urgent."
She slammed the door and clutched her small suitcase to her chest.
She barked, "I'm not here." Not this time. No.
This was her escape, and it was final.

What she'd packed into that valise would get him out of her for good.

The Stone
Rachel Westwood

You saw me first, walking with your pack, hunger in your eyes
those eyes urged me to follow and I did, the lamb that I was.
You were searching for the broken and the lost, the innocent and the
sweet.
And my Mother had never told me of the ways of men.

Tall and mysterious coloured rags of patchouli and hair of a warrior, I
followed behind.
Your cunning smile drew me to your lair, a squat of hash smoke and
chaos of both magical and bleak.
We spoke without words, your eyes burning straight through me as I
tried to hide in yesterday's school shirt.

Drunk now, as you spoke in whispers, with a flash of your gleaming
teeth.
You untied the knotted bodice of my chest, where you took my heart
and placed a stone.
I thought the furious butterflies beating in terror at my stomach were
love.
For no one had told me the ways of the wolf.

Our paths would cross for two solar years, your appetite grew, as did
my silence.
With the passing of time, that stone weighed me down, my rag doll
limbs grew tired.
But the wolf pack were hungry, you tried to share my sweetness, in
the depths of your paralysing spell,
I found a voice and timidly said 'No.'
So you took me aside with blackened eyes and punished me
ferociously.
After two solar years, I cried silently for the first time, after you left me
there,

Faced down and broken in dirty carpet burn.

I remember how, much later, I softly slipped back into the room,
where you lay in slumber among your friends
I sat and I stared, until the tears stopped flowing and rage filled my
hot stinging eyes.
I glared at the sleeping beast with that sly grin, still engraved upon
your chiselled face.
From the girl taken, eaten and spat out, emerged a woman enraged,
a woman taunted, used and left on the ground with yesterday's
mess.

And I remember how the raw light of day scorched my eyes with
shame, and you were gone.
With the passing of time, that stone weighed me down, oh how it
weighed me down.
My broken body had become my broken mind, a beaten-up box of
secret shame and anger and mistrust.
I cut into my arms to awaken my numb heart and break the ties of
rage.
But that stone still weighed me down.
That stone still weighed me down.

Quiet Now
Amanda Coleman

You left
And for the longest time
It was so loud

The emptiness inside of me
Left your vicious words
Ruminating off my walls
And through my core

It was so loud
The pieces of me
Screaming to be
Whole again

For years
It was so loud
But finally
It's quiet now
And I can hear
My own voice again

Suffocate
Jamie Lynn Martin

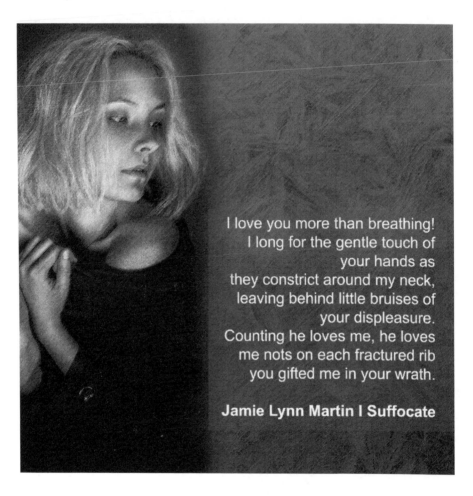

I love you more than breathing!
I long for the gentle touch of
your hands as
they constrict around my neck,
leaving behind little bruises of
your displeasure.
Counting he loves me, he loves
me nots on each fractured rib
you gifted me in your wrath.

Jamie Lynn Martin I Suffocate

Summer
Lisa Low

You always hated summer. Summer was
a shiny object on the edge of town:
you picked it up and looked around. It was
you, the desert, and the melt-down horizon.
When you said you didn't like his gun,
he hit you. When he locked you out, your
fist smashed the glass of his pick-up truck.
Even then he didn't react: your skin pushed
back like a lip, and blood poured from you,
smoking, like heaven. You said you would kill
for love, even yourself. Summer was a
cat run over. Your body in a chair,
swiveling toward the news. Summer was gin
before noon, one finger in the cookie
jar, and one in the throat. A man hitting
you. A woman pulling the doors and the
windows shut, like staircases drawn up, and
a porthole high above her for seeing
clouds. Summer was the red guts thwapping from
the split open undersides of hogs. It
was nuclear war, fiery rain, and
dust.   It was boys playing war and girls inside
playing school--because the skirts lined up with
the pants, meant something better to do.

Flight
LM

In that precise moment
when I finally knew

that I

      would not be

your bitch,
your punching bag,
and not ever your princess

(which quite possibly I always did know,
but just not sufficiently

to untangle myself
from the scenario that you insisted
was the only possible reality),

in that precise moment,
I was walking away so fast
that I took flight,
becoming what you would not allow.

The Quilt
Robin Anna Smith

> torture games
> he convinces me
> to comply

It was a yearlong ordeal. My long-time friend-turned-boyfriend-turned-ex began stalking and threatening me after I broke up with him. He had been going out, getting messed up on drugs, and having sex with other people. He was starting to frighten me with his behavior and I didn't want to get an STD.

The night after we broke up. I snuck out of my house to go talk to our friend, Eddie. The three of us had been best friends for a long time, and I wanted his take on things as I was distraught over breaking it off with Erik. Discussing it with him, I felt much better. The changes in Erik's behavior weren't all in my head, as he had suggested—Eddie was distancing himself from him too because of the erratic behavior.

After we were done talking, I slipped out his window and headed back to my vehicle. Erik jumped out from behind a bush and slammed me backward onto the car hood. He accused me of cheating on him and told me if he couldn't have me, no one could. He tore open the crotch of my pants and raped me. I was too stunned to yell for help and could barely breathe as his forearm was positioned across my throat. When he was done, he threatened to do it again if I spoke to anyone about it. I just got in my car and drove home.

After that, he would show up at my school and work regularly to intimidate me. I felt like no matter where I went, he was watching. Eventually, he graduated to breaking into my home at night through our back door to harass and rape me, sometimes at gunpoint. My mother and brother were both just feet away, asleep in their bedrooms. He told me he'd kill them if made any noise.

I got to the point where I was hypervigilant every moment of the day, and rarely slept at night because I was just waiting to be attacked again. My parents, friends, and teachers probed me for information about my change in mood. I was terrified to say anything, afraid of what he might do.

> people full
> of assumptions
> pregnant teen

Because of the stress I was under and the lack of sleep, I became physically ill in addition to depressed. My mom took me to the doctor and he recommended a psychiatrist. I went to the psychiatrist a few times, in hopes that he would be able to help me figure out what to do, but I could never figure out a way to talk to him about it indirectly. Eventually, he brought up the subject of sexual abuse and I got so scared that I never returned. Afraid to explain why I stopped going to my mother, I never mentioned it, and pretended to still be attending my appointments.

Eventually, I became pregnant. This made Erik happy because he felt no one would want me in that condition. I couldn't imagine bringing this up to my family, so I talked to Eddie, telling him it had been from someone else, and he went with me to Planned Parenthood. Unfortunately, by the time I went, I was already too far along. My only option was to have the baby.

One of the best and worst days of my life was the day I gave birth. Erik acted as if he had ruined me and he was satisfied with himself. It signaled the beginning of the end of his obsession with me. While he continued to show up unannounced and in the middle of the night, it was much less frequent and he didn't force me to have sex anymore.

Although relieved to be rid of him, I was also filled with an indescribable emptiness. Though finally able to reclaim my body, I was a changed person, mentally and physically. While I couldn't bear to keep his baby, I still felt like a part of me was taken away, leaving me incomplete.

    adopted daughter
    I wonder what
    her name is

An earlier version of this piece was published in Rhythm & Bones, Issue Two, October 2018

The Night Illaya Came Home
Nandini Sen Mehra

Concentric memories orbit like vultures
her mouth tastes of carrion,
velvet butterflies, they melt on her finger tips
she turned letting people off the hook into a fine art,
over coffee, two small sugars please, thank you,
so fucking civilized.
Shime waza, he had murmured in her ear,
panic was a brass candle stand,
just outside reach, always outside reach,
run, run when you can
while your legs are strong.
He would admire the line of muscle that ran down her calves, make
her flex for him,
pirouette like a ballerina, a slice of apple between her teeth,
she in his tee shirt that smelt of home
Norah on the radio and coffee.
When had it all come undone?
Afterwards, he admired his work on her skin, stroked her hair, called
her beautiful, called her his, her pain was her love, he had said; did
she understand?
It's all play, just play.
Run goddammit but the birds of prey, they know, they never leave.
Until that night, a window cracked open, and she awoke to see a line
of vultures perched on her windowsill - a little girl between them,
Illaya, her own name, the little girl came to her,
cupped her little hands into her bruises, and splashed it laughing,
onto the walls, over and over again,
watched it stain her clothes, drip down her face,
viscous ink gurgling out of her skin, bathing her, running down her
breasts, her thighs, squelching between her toes,
and finally,
she laughed, bitter tears that would not stop.

110

She lay her head down on the little girl's lap and sang a song that
had no words,
and so they stayed,
until the first breath of dawn,
when as one flight, with a great flapping of wings the birds rose to the
sky,
Illaya between them,
and as she watched them leave,
she dipped her fingers into the pools of ink,
she began to write.

Shime waza is a chokehold.

Immortality
Robin Anna Smith

the lion paces the fence line   canned hunt

I can see my hand shaking out of the corner of my eye. You're sifting through your bag. I look you over. Dark greasy tendrils of hair. Sharp angles of a jaw and nose. Tall, gangly body that you slouch one minute and puff up the next, like an overcorrection.

white flag   the deer scents a wolf

I can feel you hovering over me. The look in your drugged-up eyes, the smell of cigarettes, cheap booze, and ether, the drips of sweat from your face pressed into me. I feel my body giving way as you throw me onto the floor, your hands on my throat, ready to crush out my life like a roach under your boot.

field sport   the shooter claims his trophy

Guilt, as I think about the others you probably hurt after me—events which could have been prevented if I'd spoken up sooner. You should have been in jail. Even after you left me alone, I couldn't process those events, let alone talk about them with someone else.

an antelope escapes the cheetah   endurance race

It's been thirty years since you stopped stalking me. Every few years, I spend hours checking the internet for any signs of you. This is despite having read the police report about your death over twenty years ago. Part of my brain knows you can't harm me now. Other parts will always be watching for you.

Originally published in Rhythm & Bones, Issue Two, October 2018

I Hear a Robin Sing
Rachael Z. Ikins

I can't see anything. I grab at twisted nightgown wrapped around my neck, over my face.

"You want to fuck?" Her voice yells. "I'll fuck you!" She shoves me toward the bed. It is high, a new style mattress. Catches the small of my back. I gasp for air, fingernails snap on fabric. I hear it rip as her muscular knee forces my thighs apart. I am crying.

"NO! NO! " my voice cracks. Our bedroom window open, it is spring. A thought flies through my head, can neighbors hear? She always worries what they think. She sees herself: perfectly coiffed, nails filed sharp, made-up, a creased-pants example of the-only-way-to-be. If they do hear us, it will be my fault. It is warm outside, light, evening air scented with the lilac hedge alongside our house. I hear a robin sing. I used to love to ride my bike after supper when I was a kid, this kind of evening.

I kept the nightie over ten years. Its faded pink and lavender fabric rips in two, now a rag. I heave my hips,   at her. She punches one sharp-tipped hand inside me. I'm still screaming NO NO NO. Somehow I slide out from under her.

"Get the fuck away from me!" she hollers. I'm the attacker? She will be sure of it later. I stagger to the bathroom. Shield my breasts one-handed, throw the door lock. Sometimes she tackles doors like a football player. They explode open. Other times she slams them, pictures on both sides of walls fall, glass breaks.

I put my hand between my legs to see, is there blood? I sink to the cool tiled floor. The nightgown was white with roses printed on. I hold a scrap to my face. Blot my tears. I hear the television come on, Access Hollywood. My little dog snuffles along the door-crack. I want to let him in. I can't move yet. He thumps his body down on the other side to wait.

One day soon I will leash him and his sister, stuff cat in carrier, throw my medications and important legal papers in my computer bag, grab purse and cell phone, we will leave.

We will stay with friends while I find us an apartment. I will sign divorce papers and explain to my passionate young attorney that I do not care what I am entitled to, I will no longer fight her for anything at all, not even a dollar bill. We will move into our new place end of July. Helpers will leave us, four survivors afloat, a sea of cardboard. A friend and daughter will bring me a plate of chocolate chip cookies tied with a turquoise and orange bow. " Happy Home Coming."

It will take me two years to stop flinching when I hear neighbors on the stairway, to stop expecting the locked security door to blast open. It will take me two years to decide to write about it, to take the closet door off its hinges so the bully has no where to hide. She will have stalked me from the back seat, her friends' Lincoln, searching the parking lot while I stood right next to the poop can with my dogs.

She will knock on my door, winter. Not knowing who it is, I will open. The dogs will attack her legs. She will thrust my painting and a box of small treasures into my hands. Spin away, dash downstairs into the snow. I learn to be in charge of the lock. There is a huge difference to a life where you are in charge. Today I will walk the dogs into fresh spring air. Starlings chortle from poplar budded branches.

Epilogue: one day I see her on a metal bench outside Bed, Bath & Beyond. Without my glasses I recognize the crease in the woman's sneaker socks and realize it is my ex. I enter the store, make my purchase, leave the doors at an angle that prevents me from seeing the bench again. I shake my head. She is just a white-haired old woman, bouncing one leg. No longer dyes her hair. I drive away, into my freedom.

"I Hear a Robin Sing" was published by the feminist journal S/tick in their winter issue 2017 called "Repeat Defenders." Thanks to editor Sarah Jean Krahn. –Rachael Ikins

"I decided to take part in this hugely important anthology because after many years I still question myself, it became a deeply hidden weight of shame which yet somehow is with me every day and has in part moulded me into my adult self. I felt it would be healthy to speak out, for myself and for all those who are voiceless and hurting."

Rachel Westwood

Could I Forgive?
Jane Basil

I am a sentient being,
a human,
when it began
I was not yet a woman.

Whatever my species, sex or age,
there can be
no
excuse.

Should I forgive you?
Lay to rest each punch and kick,
those thick fists driven into my belly,
the long scar that parts my hair,
the squelching mechanism in your head
which submitted the order to smash me,
to mash cigarettes in my face
to rape me whenever you felt the urge
to hurl me against walls,
throw me down stairs?
Should I forgive your base rage
or your indifference
when I lay still and silent,
staining the rug while the dust settled?
Panicked plans of escape
sprayed from your lips
like scared chicken shit
that time you thought I was dead.

Should I forgive the attacks on my mind;
the treacherous threats
of death to my kin

if I had the temerity to rebel;
to spill your filthy secrets
and beg somebody for help?
Should I forgive the vile stink
you injected into my stretched flesh?
I hear you are ill and soon you will die
should I show compassion and rush to your side
denying your guilt?
Should I forgive you?
Should I?
Should I?
And could I, if I tried?

Maybe, since you failed to break me,
but I cannot forgive the stains you left
on those less able to survive.

There was No One To Tell
Kindra Austin

Who was I supposed to tell? His mother?

Ring, ring, ring...

Hello?

Hey Mom. Just wanted to let you know that your precious son fucked me in the ass last night after I'd passed out from drinking way too fucking much. Yeah, I'd finally given in, and accompanied him to the titty-bar. Don't pretend you don't know what I'm talking about—I'm always complaining about him going to the clubs. Yes, I'm certain he fucked me in the ass. I'm sore and bleeding. It's something he's always wanted, but has consistently been denied. Last night I passed out, like I said, and he took what he wanted.

Who was I supposed to tell? The police?

Ring, ring, ring...

911, where's your emergency?

Blah, blah, blah. Please send the cops to arrest my husband for fucking me in the ass. We went out last night to the titty-bar, and we both got fucking shit-faced. I woke up this morning with a bleeding anus—I'm pretty sure my husband fucked me in the ass after I'd passed out. I'm definitely not okay with being fucked in the ass, especially while unconscious. My husband raped me. Yes I'm sure I was unconscious. Yes, I do know that Michigan is one of thirteen states that make ridiculous exceptions for marital rape. Believe me, he's reminded me of his rights.

Who was I supposed to tell? My dad?

Ring, ring, ring...

Hello?

Daddy, my husband raped me. Yes, I called the police. It's complicated...difficult to prove. We were both drunk. He took me to a topless club. Yes, I agreed to go, but...no, nothing funny happened while we were there. We just kept drinking, and he kept throwing money at the dancers. I drove us home, I think...I don't remember. But I know I went to bed with my clothes on. I woke up without any pants, and I was bleeding. Yes, I'm sure I was dressed when I went to bed. Daddy, please don't judge me, just help me.

Goddamn it, I know I was dressed when I went to bed that night. I also know I was bleeding when I woke up, naked from the waist down. I was a *married* woman, assaulted by my *husband*.
I was assaulted by the one man who I should have been able to trust above anyone else. I know I'm not the only one who has experienced this level of betrayal.

I never feared death
Marilyn Rea Beyer

I never feared death
Until you died.

Now – again – I fear facing you
With your dark curls and your Sinatra sneer.

Like on my 28th birthday when you warned to me watch my weight,
"Or I'll trade you in for two 14s."

And then you actually did.
More than two, really.

You mocked my other lovers as "nice boys,"
Then taught me toxic lessons.

Yes, you made my blood rush,
Grabbed me by the waist and hissed, "Follow me."

Who's your jitterbug partner now?
Do you make the tender angels cry?
Do you do to them what you did to Bernadette?

I wish sometimes I did believe in Hell
So I could just let you go.

That frail gray man who died last year did not resemble you.

People said how much you'd changed. Really?
Enough to apologize?
Enough to quench my fear of Heaven?

His Name is David
Melita White

My rapist's name is David
Not the one who fought Goliath
My rapist has no courage
Not the everyday Davids
The ones that you might know
I'm sorry he has the same name
I'm sorry if your David is nice
Not all Davids are rapists
But mine was, yes
The David who raped me
Is not my cousin
Who is always friendly
With crinkly eyes
His name is David too
Nor my uncle
Who tells the best stories
And has lived an interesting life
And certainly not my Dad's best friend
Who I've known since birth
He is a sweet and gentle man
There are so many Davids
And only one of them raped me
The David who raped me
I renamed Asshole
Twenty-five years ago
It felt right and fitting
To dehumanise a monster
Yet every time I said it
(Many thousands of times)
It felt like spewing bile
A green-yellow acid
A chaser to the vomit

Of his name
Asshole
But cursing kept him hidden
A shadow, a swear word
Until it marked my soul
Leaving stains like his semen
Which he forced me to swallow
That burnt my wet soft throat
And tinted it with fear
A crusty yellow substance
On my milky white breasts
A cracking stinky mask
Barely concealing his hatred
His ownership of me
I remember:
The cold of the toilet seat
Goose pimples on my arse
My bodysuit snapped open
At the crotch by his fingers
Giving in to his will
With deadness in my head
Mute limpness in my limbs
I was a thing to use up
His knowing grin and laugh
That twinkle in his eye
A psychopath's pleasure
In knowing that he'd had me
My rapist's name is David
And some of you might know him
In telling you his name
I open up the box
The fear was never mine
I let the shame float out
It soars and it mingles with fresh air

Exorcism
Lola White

Dutifully I hug him,
walk him to his car.
Before he's gone a block,
I scrub his after-shave
from my cheek.

In a frenzy,
I strip his sheets
from the hide-a-bed,
stuff them into the washer,
sprinkle baking soda
on the mattress,
convinced it reeks of him.

I toss out the soggy papers
his dog pee'd on,
dip a mop in Lysol,
wash the floor.
I wipe down every surface;
it's madness, but I must
perform these ablutions
or I will drown.

Despite the January chill,
I fling open all the windows.
My teenage son stares,
open-mouthed.
I catch his eye, my shrug
a plea for indulgence.

I'm ashamed, ashamed
of my father, ashamed

of my shame.
I pray with every molecule
that I will never give this young man,
whom I love utterly,
reason or need
to scour my ghost from his rooms.

Offering
Sabrina Escorcio

touch dulls over time
as fingertips run cold
across tender flesh,
and vacant thought
consumes the desire
that once burned
under the surface
of his skin

for I, once again
have become
less than enough,
so, I gather even now
broken pieces of self
left behind by man
as an offering
to the next.

To Hate What You Know
Tiffany K Elliot

Sip my bitter cordial, mix the gall and be drunk
on my voidness, on the body-turned-fruit, forbidden
and deadly.

I am blank and empty,
a cracked carafe—filled with the bile
that spills onto stained bedsheets.

Fermented away
all sweetness—now I stand
cacti-barbed and empty, thirst-starved,
aching.

You expected me to fall like a glass
drawn to the center of the world.

I can't say no. I can't
exist in your arms.

So give me your mingled water
and blood, fill my broken cask.
Let me drain you the way you—
all of you—have always drained me.

The Pros and Cons of Being This Heavily Medicated
Georgia Park

With humans being predators
and the females of the species
doubling as prey
our brains are hard wired
to scan for faces
I used to see his every day

In the grains of the forest
cut down in pieces, sawed into halves
and sanded to make up our living room table
and in the beer puddles, which to me
looked rainbow but don't anymore

now that my diet consists
of white, chalky skittles
and i am marshmallowed
to the teeth, i don't see
the faces like I used to
mostly i just fall asleep

I do remember just one tree
I'd carved some initials into
with a knife i don't feel the need
to carry around anymore
but i can't remember the names
and i don't think they'd come to me again

even without the medication
because it wasn't a face
all i could manage
to create at that time was
a scraggly little heart shape

It Was Tragic
Rachel Finch

It was tragic,
the way we clung
to dreams and longings,
the way they smothered
the trauma with labels
and tried to squeeze
our psyche into straightjackets
too small to bound the inner.
It was tragic,
the way we retreated to our
subconscious and made homes
of the fortresses that
housed the ancient but
remembered.
It was tragic,
the way we sparked up,
chewed Valium to
numb the yesterdays and
mauled at any euphoria
we could claim.

Flesh
Amanda Coleman

You left this
Taste in my mouth
That I couldn't rinse away
And every time
I'd try to swallow it down
The poison would sink
A little deeper
Until the fill of you
Ate me away
Like a parasite
From the inside out
Leaving me with
Holes to my surface
And all this
Flesh to heal

Family Night
Georgia Park

I sped to the poetry reading
like it was AA and I was on the verge of relapsing.
The theme of the night was family.
She said, "Mama knew daddy
was coming into my room." She looked
at us, and we nodded.
Then she sang the blues.
He said, "My father turned out
to be a sex offender
i was just trying to find
a way to forgive him
when he told me not to visit
so now, i have nothing."
I sat in the back but was spotted
"Georgia! Welcome back!
Oh, I see a darkness rising-
You should always come to us when that happens!
Would you like to read something?"
"Nah, I'm here to listen."
they reminded me again and again
that they are my friends, family even
which is good, cause i have trouble keeping track
of who can be trusted and who just can't.

Untied
Laurie D. Wise

There is a darkness tied up inside
Breaching the boundaries
Captivity amplified
It's difficult to breath
Contaminating me
Skin and bones
With no one home
But for all
That should not be spoken
Teetering on the edge
Elaborate steps to prevent malice
From being woken
These are the secrets I keep
Lest a stir, a face, a sound, a place
Startles the unavowed
So I tip toe around myself
And everyone else
Perpetually panicked
Cutting and drinking and starving
To leak it out, drown it out, kill it out
Time and connection has shown me
It's better to be quiet and lonely
Why is the silence so loud?
Stuck between solitude and kindness
And repressed
Brutal remembrance
If only
I hadn't grown in a box made of wood and danger
Built by strangers
They were so good at pretending to care
Hold me in your thoughts and prayers
Or please just hold me

So I don't fall apart
Like a work of abstract art
None of it fits quite right
With eyes that see what they should not
Ears only hear what they want
Hands hide truth behind your back
Hearts afraid to unpack
I'm bulging at the seams
Forsaking my dreams
Made of strings
Insidiously unraveling
Dangling
By a
Thread
Scissors whisper freedom
If I could just reach them
But I am
Shackled and shrouded
Awaiting
Life
Unclouded
And a safe space to hide
Biding time
Until I become
Untied

Little Red
Wilda W. Morris

Life is not the same
since the wolf showed his face.
I no longer dally
along the path picking daisies,
finding sheep or dogs
in the nimbus clouds,
whistling the song of robin
or cardinal. Seldom
do I traverse the route alone
and never at night. He comes
in my dreams, his hot breath
on my neck, or on grandmother's,
his cackling laughter, his leer
saying more than his lips,
his sharp teeth ready to cut holes
in my sanity. At home, sheep,
goats, even my own border collie,
take on some aspect of the elongated
chin, deep-set eyes, teeth or tongue
of that wolf. Though safe, I shudder.

Originally published in The Homestead Review.

Smoke & Mirrors
Laurie D. Wise

Divinity reaches down from the sky, or maybe right up through the ground, there really isn't any way to tell, it happens so fast, the rug gets pulled out from under me, my soul is wearing thin and my heart is quaking from everything unknown. The sun isn't really rising and setting, we're spinning around in an unstable atmosphere and that scares the fuck out of me. I don't know where I'm supposed to be and if I just keep running I'll only end up tired or right back where I started. I'm scared to stop because I'll surely die, end up in the sky or underground, and become part of everything unknown, it's hard to tell. I just want to go home.

But that was washed away a long time ago,
To a place where words don't work.

Days when I was too scared, so my mind erased the parts that burnt. Days when I was in so much pain my mind locked it up and threw the key in the fire. I hope someone is waiting for me. I'm empty, I can't see, so how can I possibly be, anything else, other than a child, because so much time has been lost, beaten out of me, stolen by thieves and it has left a ripple in the fabric that is burning.

Children need looking after.

But the smoke is too thick to see if there is anyone looking after me. Flames are blowing back into my face, sweat is blurring my eyes, my skin is singed. Burning bridges that I wish I could drive my car off of but I have forgotten that my wings are melted and I haven't any surrender left, like a mirror reflecting a mirror until all that remains is rubble in the shape of life long after the bombs stopped falling and the ash has blown away. Shame creeps in and I try to build a new bridge.

Rupture and repair.
Release and restore.

Unsure who or where I will be when I finally wake up. I'd ask my friends for advice but I don't have any. They have formed a secret society that is absent of me except they aren't keeping secrets, they are hoarding denial and planning where to aim the machete for best possibility of beheading. Smoke and mirrors, disguising the sinners. I don't want to be a part of their prison anyway. I tried to climb the fence they built to keep me out and now I've been cut again, bleeding again, and they just sit back and whisper while I pour salt on my wounds. I'm sleep deprived, what else do they want from me? I forgot the chorus to my theme song, and any sense of right and wrong, another cursed charade to prolong the undeniable desire to belong.

We could cut hay,
To pass the day.

But it's dry and I am a fire made of mistaken memories. A wall no one can get through, with wicked weedy tendrils growing from my foundation. Eager to snuff anyone that gets close enough. I have no control over what they fear and you will get hurt if you come near. I'm a well-armed woman wielding no weapons, ready to leap, swan dive, and for just a moment, I am alive, free, walking in waist deep water that gets deeper each day as I weep for humanity and hang on to the fumes that are left

With my

Hummingbird

Heart.

Persona Poem- Helen Martins
Petru Viljoen

Helen, Helen, why did you hide?
> *I, who walked obliquely*
> *(they cut off my little toes)*
> *was a daytime furtive*
> *a wizened, furrowed, wrinkled wraith-*
> *I danced my shadow selves at night naked*

Helen, Helen, why did you cry?

> *Ugly and dirty long before*
> *I lived even though I was pretty. The*
> *serving and the serving. The serving made*
> *me cry. Before she and he and he and the baby died.*

Helen, Helen, what did you create?

> *First thing I did was throw out the stove. Ha!*
> *After that long night, the business with the*
> *(lack of) light, the protracted shudder of grey*
> *existence. Apprehended for the time. I. Being.*
> *Owl.*

> *Living the numinous night*
> *light uniquely intended, acutely created*
> *the social realm transcended*

> *an enigmatic conception of*
> *Biblical proportion*
> *I, tiny, wiry sparrow so called.*

> *Three hours in counted normal time it took*
> *lighting lamps, candles. The night. The ritual.*
> *Softening. The ridicule.*

Helen, Helen, how did you live?

*I lived by the spoon put by the making of the
unspawned being, nourishment incomplete
I stayed and loved and others fed. Me. When I
let them.*

*I lived by tremendous surge of suppressed
hunger. Amidst banal accepted routine of
them who said they will like me. Be like us.
And I? Couldn't.*

Helen, Helen, how did you die?

*I died as I lived. By my own hand(s), shredded,
bared to crushed glass. Pierced,
punctured, consumed right through.
My ashes were in red. The owl was left
unburdened.*

Survival in Waves
Elizabeth Beaver

We all remember,
that moment in childhood,
when we first felt,
with bated breath,
that beautiful shining something,
slip through our grasping hand,
like the tired waves,
of the tremulous tide.

And knew in that weary
moment,
it was gone forever,
that is what it's like,
to be a survivor,
but the feeling never goes
away,
it just ebbs and flows,
like the tired waves,
of the tremulous tide.

Kissing the stars

Jamie Lynn Martin

Do you ever wonder what it feels like to
kiss the stars?
To stare at the moon asking for its
forgiveness.
What does it feel like to breathe on
command
when your lungs forget how to sing?
When the world seems so dark,
and the only light left is the fire in his eyes.
How can I wash away this unchaste sin
that has seeped into my skin,
so unwillingly thrust upon me?
How do I tell the moon my words are
dripping with sour milk,
left out by his misdeed?
How do you ever kiss the stars if your
mouth is filled with bees?
When your screams are muffled by the
stinging left on your
tongue.

Jamie Lynn Martin I Kissing the stars

140

Bodies In The Graveyard
Sarah Doughty

"My body was never a temple,
but a graveyard. And every grave has
a demon to call home."

My body was never a temple, but a graveyard. One of those long forgotten fields, scattered with centuries-old tombstones. Some so weathered with time that the names are no longer legible. Some so stained from years of neglect. And the grounds have overgrown with vines and weeds, leaving some graves invisible.

This is how my body remembers all I've endured. Some scars are so deep, they've been covered through time. Some are just inside. And these demons of mine. They each have a grave to call their home.

They haunt me.

Branded
Meg Baines

She looked at the leaves, and the colours they bled,
and wished her soul could do the same, inside it's brown and dead.
The gray sky reflected her mood, it all replayed in her mind,
The thought of you still seared her with a painful, lucid bind.
Inane conversations that suddenly exploded,
And all the while you would claim that you were goaded.
Some days are easier than others, when she's reminded of the truth,
That not all men are equal, and you're the breathing proof.
Twisted corridors of lies, all she craved for was clear air,
And even though now years have passed, the scars she still bares.

In a Time of Crisis
Amanda J. Forrester

I punch myself.

When it is time
I do not act.

Allow me to demonstrate:
I laugh on the outside
to make you feel better.

I am exhausted from faking it.

My survival depends
on my imagination.

There will not always be time.
I realize this.

When I finally see a break in the weather,
I will run.

But I will never tell.

I Fasted for the Flies
Amanda J. Forrester

No one expected what the wolves would bring.
Houseflies hover, cover the bodies.
When the first kid dies,
to celebrate, they pound the beers.

Peeking out from the sheet
(names removed to protect the guilty)
Do you remember this trend?
It'd be great if you could
stop blaming the dead.

Which side are you on?
The difference
between the sun and a full moon:
one you can walk on,
the other you hide from.

I only want to hide,
not save the world
or even one person.   not even me
There is no capturing
a tsunami in a thimble.

I should try a new look, they say.
There are eight things my eyes
are trying to tell me. Eight things
I am running from.

I am not interested in the cause
not anymore –
just the symptoms
and new eyeliner will fix that up.

Forget the past, try something new.
Upload your latest selfie.
Smile.
If only I learned to cry.

"This anthology is important to me because for years I
carried so much anger inside me, angry that no one
Protected me, angry that when I spoke up I was pushed a
side & ignored. Unless you've been through it, you have
no idea what that does to a child, but from some of my
darkest moments there is now light shed, a silence that
has been broken by many through the power of words, &
art. Writing is my therapy to be able to heal & express
what was kept hidden inside, but also to help others.

The silence needed to be broken, this anthology helps
bring us together to do so."

Madame K Poetess

Unlearning
Irma Do

I learned in the back seats of cars
The alcoves of bars
How to please
And how to tease.
I learned at the department store
How to dress to settle the score.
And underneath, my angel side
Learned how to cause a great divide.
A push, a pinch, a tug, a spin
Put pain to the side; upfront, just grin.
I learned my worth, a ratio
Of tits and ass and let it go.
And when you think the game is done,
You spy your girls and know they've won.
Those weren't lessons, they were deceit.
I was fooled, their greatest feat.
Should I just acquiescent to my defeat?

Oh hell no.
#metoo
#timesup

Painted Thighs
Rachel Finch

Lay me down and pretend men
of all colours haven't
painted their own shade of
rainbow on my thighs.

Rachel Finch | Painted Thighs

I'm Trying
Christie L. Starkweather

When I flinch at your touch
And push against your embrace
Please understand
The demons I face
And it's not that I don't want
You to hold me at night
It's that the last one I loved
Never loved me quite right
Their touch was not gentle
Their embrace was not warm
They left my soul broken
As my body bled on the floor
But I'm trying
Dear God am I trying
To just let you in
And open my heart
To loving somebody again.

CLS Poetry by Christie L. Starkweather | I'm Trying

Constellations
Dena M. Daigle

If I drew a map for you across my body, one made entirely of stars marking all of the places ever violated by human hands, my bones would be wrapped in a galaxy made of flesh.
A pink protostar would mark the spot where my innocence was once sacred and pure;
and those tiny flecks of stardust due north would represent the seeds of my womb that never got to bloom.
The black hole covering my mouth would portray the silent screams and pleas for help that were written all over my face, yet no one heard.
And the supernova adorning my chest would depict the moment that my heart exploded into millions of pieces because no one would save me.
I'd draw the blue supergiant, Rigel, and its star cluster family to represent the bruises left across my throat by those who hoped to silence me.
And if the stars didn't paint the picture vividly enough, I would sketch a grid around my head to show you the way the fabric of time seems to fold in on itself and repeat in infinite loops of pain.
You see, this is the map leading to the little girl who lost her sense of direction once upon a time in the Milky Way.
So if I showed you the way to my soul, would you love me enough to trace my constellations, or would you simply look the other way?

The Carapace
Melita White

Her army is formidable
It surrounds and protects her
In the open field
In which she stands
Alone and wild
While encircled by legions
Her army is en garde
She has trained them
To expect the enemy
To be ever vigilant
To trust no-one
And to always fight
To always defend
She is vividly vulnerable
A distressed damsel
Dressed in white
Pale hair streaming
Eyes wide darting
Feet pace nervously
Breath ever quickening
The enemy is close
Her army encloses her
Cold and hard
Chain mail armour
Metal helmets
Gleaming and repellant
Her army forms a steel fortress
Spikes ready
Pointing outwards
The imminent danger
Approaches always

Flinch
Megha Sood

My soul flinches at the
very mention of your name
My fingers tremble in the night
as I recall the nightmare
recursively
like a bad movie,
stuck on the reels
I want to scrape the
memory of yours
want to mask it with the
empty memories of
my life
the stench of your
sickening presence
has suffocated me
for so long
has left an abyss in my soul
even if I'm blinded
by the goodness
of the light surrounding me
you still can manage
to cast a shadow
and eclipse my heart
with all the pain
I have been
hiding all along
the shivering, trembling
and those seizures of
incessant pain
never seems to slow down
the gut-wrenching
feel of your touch

which scarred my soul
has left a deep impression
which I so want to ignore
Not a single day passes
when I wish your
existence should
be a glitch
in nature
fixing the mistake of
an excuse for a human you are
and everything I hope for
becomes pure and true again
and I forever wake up from the
the bad dream that you are.

This Room is Not for Rent
Christine E. Ray

The Greek chorus has declared me
damaged beyond repair
incapable of a "normal" life
"better off dead" say the well-meaning citizens
than "broken"
preferring the image of the golden haired innocent child angel
comforted by a merciful God
over the living angry woman
who refuses to be silent
I try not to let these voices
rent space in my head
they are destructive tenants
who forfeit their security deposit
scrawl graffiti in red lipstick on my walls
dirty
shameful
Lolita
guilty
complicit
whore
bitch
I try not to buy into the vitriol
when they imply that my life has no meaning
that I am an abomination
a red, raw, bleeding thing they deem too unseemly to look at
unfit for polite society
"Fuck You!" I want to shout at the top of my lungs with my hands
covering my ears
Some days it is hard to find the armor of my rage
when I am just so god damned tired
of having to prove over and over again
that I am worthy of continued existence

that I deserve to walk this earth
breathe the oxygen
as if I am the one who must continue to do penance
for other's sins

Blame
Nikita Goel

When a little girl loses her virginity to a stranger who
Tore her apart and feasted upon her like a piece of meat,
They are going to blame the little girl
"Oh, she should not walk alone at nights"
"She was wearing a dress that asked for it"
"It was her boyfriend."
Maybe, we should blame the Mothers of the daughters,
Who forgot to teach their daughters how to breathe fire and burn
everything to ashes?
The mothers who never told their daughters that they hold within
themselves
A little bit of the sun, the stars and the sky.
Maybe, we should blame the Mothers of the sons
Who raised those men and encouraged them to become monsters.
The mothers who set a live example of why is it okay for men to walk
all over the woman and never apologize for it.
Maybe, we should blame the Fathers of the daughters.
Who never told their daughters that they could become anyone they
wanted to be
Who raised them to be slaves to their husbands and sons,
thereafter?
Maybe, we should blame the Fathers of the sons.
Who got drunk and looked at other women with lustful eyes
Who told their sons that girls carry venom in their blood, which is
thrown out through the uterus every month?
Maybe, we should blame the wives of those men,
Who do not walk away when a man tells them that her womb did not
create a life but his fluid did.
Who let a man tell her every day that she is living on his mercy?

Abused and Alone

F.I. Goldhaber

Alone in the dark,
hoping the swelling
will subside and the
bruises will heal, that
blood will stop flowing
and the broken bones
will knit themselves back
together on their
own. Not waiting but
surviving. Living.
Longing for escape
even though you have
nowhere to run, no
place to hide, nothing
to spend for food or
clothing or shelter.

Haunted all your days
by the conviction,
planted in your minds
by perpetrators,
that you are to blame
for being abused.
Suffering from the
physical damage,
mental battering,
and emotional
repercussions for
the rest of your lives.

Others ask why you
did not fight back, why

you did not stand up
to your abusers.
That victim blaming
just adds more shame
to your suffering and
preys on your anguish.

So you will spend your
lives alone, taught from
childhood that you are
unworthy of love.

Asking For It
Sarah Doughty

"Before you point that accusatory finger
in my direction, remember this:
I never asked for it."

The sun is setting and I feel the cold seeping into my bones. I feel
the life bleeding out of my feet, leeching into the ground. And I stand
here, breathing smoke into the sky. Because that's all I have left to
give — pieces of my broken spirit. And that's all that remains after
the vultures picked me apart. So before you point that accusatory
finger in my direction, remember this: I never asked for it. I never
gave the wrong signals. I didn't deserve all you forced upon me.

And how could I have known better? I was barely old enough to walk,
let alone understand what vile things you wanted from me. If you
wouldn't blame a child, then why blame the teenager for going to a
party? Why blame the woman that was followed home from work?
It's time everyone takes a hard look at the patterns. Those men saw
something they wanted, and they took it. With complete disregard for
their victim. And I suppose that's part of the point. They have the
power. They need it. So they take it wherever they can get it.

So, if you are a victim, and you've ever felt that finger pointing in your
direction, know that no matter what anyone tells you — You. Are.
Not. To. Blame.

Truth or Fiction
Claire, from CK words and thoughts

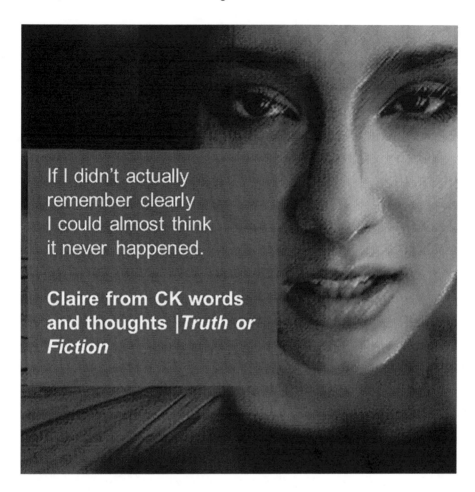

If I didn't actually remember clearly I could almost think it never happened.

Claire from CK words and thoughts |*Truth or Fiction*

I Remember
Rachel Finch

I'm thirty-six weeks pregnant, lying on my back in the labour ward, three doctors in a three and a half hour period force their fingers inside me to check my dilation and I remember.
I'm fourteen hours into labour when they decide to cut me to 'make it easier' and the room swallows me whole, spits me out, 7 years old and I remember.
I'm four hours post labour, tiny baby girl lying beside me, too weak from lack of blood to move, curled up and seeing stars, blood leaking from between my legs and I remember.
No moment has been sacred.

Garavel
Jessie Michelle

I drop to the ground.
Gravel beneath my feet,
and now the bed I lay in.
Stuck in a moment
that was forced upon me.
Stuck in a memory
I am only just now remembering.
It haunts me.
The flashes.
Lightening after the storm.
Trying to remember and forget
at the same time.
The rain falls.
It doesn't stop.
But it's never enough to clean me.
Never enough to wash away
the aftermath;
the destruction.
I sit inside my memories.
Trying to put together the puzzle
that is built of my confusion.
But I am living in a world
with only three corner pieces.
Incomplete.
Unsolved.
I am a piece of art
that will never be finished.
I am forever connected to you
in a way I don't fully understand.
I try to mend the cracks I have
fallen into,
but they have grown a

little wider with time.
Hard to ignore.
Impossible to escape

"Bred of fear and depravity and groomed by denial, rape culture will continue to thrive unless we rip it from its roots, expose it to the elements and let it wither until it returns to the earth as dust. I add my story to our collective voice to plant seeds of new growth.
Imagine what might bloom in fields fertilized by unbridled consent."

Rachel Kobin

162

She
Ali Grimshaw

She learned to take herself
out of her body, to separate
no longer be encased by flesh.
She learned to go, bundle her spirit
carry it out and away, above invasion
the uninvited intolerable penetration.
She learned numbness, not to be
within her skin, to pack up her
soul and exit, just until it was over.
She learned how,
survival was her teacher.
It was the only way.
She didn't know help
with mouth stitched closed
only endurance walked with her.

The Scars Inside
Julie A Malsbury

If mental illness left physical scars,

Would OCD callous my hands
thicker still and heavier each time
I touch, count, sort, resort,
recount, and count again, or wipe,
wash, fold, refold, until the edges align,
or check just one more time,

just one more, that the light was out,
the oven off, the door locked,
keys in the keys bowl,
and lunch packed for tomorrow,
so I don't forget like the last time
and all the times before?

Would anxiety encircle my neck
in tightly cut, fine lacy patterns,
filigree reminders of failure after failure?

And panic rush out from ribs
and sternum, cleave my chest open
to jab my heart with pikes and sticks
until it hardly dares to flutter.

Would ADD appear unwanted
and without warning, as a rash
or breakout resistant to every shower
scrub, cream, and chemical peel?

and surface in new places
to leave behind pockmarks,

tiny, tell-tale divots and and large trenches
trekked across my body.

Would PTSD swirl
around my ears
along my jaw,
where a lover once caressed,
but only yelled for years?

Would white snakes of scar tissue
cascade my neck, shoulders, and chest?
Darken on bad days,
and pulse with thunder?

Or deepen into craters on days
when the horn of work trucks blare
too loud and too close?

Would new scabs appear
with discovery after discovery
of each new trigger:
each dog bark, each car alarm—
my own dog, my own car—

each loud voice, or harsh tone,
when a friend, a mother, a lover
instigates tears and shaking
even when I know I am safe?

Would depression gray my hair,
limp and never clean despite shower
after shower, and shampoo after shampoo?

When I finally—finally—accept
the twisted, matted mess,

the strands stuck to my face,
tangled and knotted, a perpetual birds nest,

would it simply fall out,
strand by strand, clump by clump,
to leave the whole of me as naked
and raw as my nerves?

First Boyfriend

Lisa Low

Mostly I worry. Bad things happen to girls.
I've been over it with her many times,
wanting my wisdom to keep her from harm.
"I can protect myself!" she insists, making
a show of ferocity, asking why
I don't trust her. "It's not a matter of trust,"
I say, stroking her beautiful hair.
"It's a savage world. They may flip you on
your belly, pull your legs apart, go in
savagely, hooting with laughter. Whatever
happens, remember, you are fierce. Whatever
they do, don't let them bury you."

The Lucky Ones
Grace Alexander

I had a panic attack this morning.

A really bad one. The worst one in a long time.

Pardon me. I'll back up.

I have panic attacks sometimes.

Most of the time, I white-knuckle my way through the actual panic, and then I collapse and pant a little once I get out of the situation, and then I'm fine and no-one around me even knows I was having an attack at all.

Usually, I'm awake for the whole thing.

The really bad ones, though...

The really bad ones always start out as a dream.

The dream is very realistic. It's about me, when I was younger.

I'm simultaneously living through the events in the dream and watching them unfold from a short distance with a feeling of increasing dread.

The dream quickly turns into a nightmare. There's usually a sexual component, sometimes a violent one; but often it's just an insidious, sickening progression of events that a kid of the age I am in the dream doesn't really understand.

Of course, it's not actually a dream. That would be too easy.

The dream is really a flashback that my traitorous mind has decided I'm in a good enough place now to handle.

(That's the real kick in the taco - I only get flashbacks when things have been going really well for me, when I feel like I am adulting successfully, when I think I've exorcised my demons, when I start to wonder if maybe, just maybe, I've finally shaken loose of my past.)

Anyway.

Flashback.

I wake up sitting bolt upright and I can't stop shaking and I'm lightheaded and my breath is whistling in my throat and I am *furious*.

Because GODDAMMIT already. When is enough going to be enough?

When do I get to stop paying these taxes on something I never wanted to own?

I sit up on the edge of the bed, and I yank my sweat-soaked nightgown over my head, and I ball it up and throw it in the corner and I jam my arms and legs into my clothes and I manage to find some socks and stuff my feet in them and my face is buzzing and I think I'm going to pass out and I'm so angry, I'm so angry, I am *so angry* because I am SICK OF THIS SHIT.

I will be 42 years old in 12 days and 16 hours and 37 minutes and I'm about to fall over in a dead ass faint because of stupid fucking shit that happened almost thirty years ago and it's NOT FUCKING FAIR.

I double over on myself and count to ten, to fifteen, to twenty-five, to fifty. Breathe in, hold, breathe out.

Eventually, of course, I realize that no amount of counting or trying to make myself do stupid calming breathing exercises is going to help, and I'm disgusted with myself.

So I stand up unwillingly and make my feet walk down the hall and stick my head in the living room door to see if my wife is awake, and she basically goes from lying down on the couch typing on her laptop to standing next to me in one point two seven seconds when she sees my face because she knows something is very, very wrong.

I know. I'm pathetic.

I'm still making this weird whistling gasping noise, and I kind of sag against her and get both hands fisted in her shirt, so she half carries me into the living room and curls up around me and holds me until I manage to even out my breathing a little and some color comes back into my face.

And I'm embarrassed and grateful and pissed and relieved and humiliated all at the same time. I'm trying not to look too hard at whatever the hell just got unpacked from behind the wall in my mind (that I don't remember building but which I maintain vehemently is there for a good goddamn reason), so I just lean on her with my eyes closed and shake and blow out air like I'm a winded racehorse for a while.

After a bit, I get up and I scrub at my face and realize every muscle in my body hurts, so I grimace and complain and rotate my shoulders and shake out my wrists and rub my temples and take an Advil and I get on with my day.

Because that's what you do when you're one of the broken ones, because to do anything else is to let the goddamn fucking fuckers who did this to me win and I'll be damned if I let THAT happen.

170

I'm not special. There are hundreds of thousands of people just like me - survivors of child sex abuse - for whom the after-effects never go away.

It's the gift that keeps on giving. And giving. And giving.

But we try to forget. We live regular lives (or we fake it really, really well.)

Most of us have grown up sex (and some of us get raped again as adults, and it's kind of like welp, yeah, so THAT happened again... because for us, we always know it's a possibility.)

Quite a few of us get married (with varying levels of success), and some of us have kids of our own, and we do our best to be "normal" (whatever the fuck THAT is.)

All of us just want to feel like we belong someplace, but we're not sure there is any place for people as damaged as we are.

And a few of us are the lucky ones, and one day we find someone who is there for us even when we make weird noises and can't talk or breathe right and won't stop shaking.

They hold us, and they don't say "it's OK" (because it's not OK and never will be) but they say "I'm here. I've got you."

And that is truth and it is enough.

It has to be.

I Will Bury You
Jane Basil

It felt like the end;
I was too new to know that it was only
the beginning,
that day when I was ten,
the day that boy tried to rape me.
He'd ignored my reputation,
hadn't reckoned on my strength.
His efforts failed and his testicles
regretted the kiss from my knee, but
the world became a dirty place.

I felt tainted,
learned to hate my body

Around the same time
my father chose to desire and despise me.
He trained me to be any man's handmaiden.
I figure it was revenge
since I was the only female he knew
who refused to splay her legs for him.

It's not that he supplied the guys,
but he taught me to catch them by accident
like a fly might teach a spider
which portions taste sweet
even as it struggles not to be eaten.

He groomed me to be
a pretty little victim, a vegetarian
with the odour of a keen
man-eater.
Soon, men and boys

were wedging me into corners,
pressing angular crotches into my groin,
their lips lunging toward mine
like they were angling
for love or romance
even as they grabbed at breasts
that bulged rebelliously
under a school uniform.

At first
they were no match
for my muscle and disgust.
When I left three sprawled together in a heap
I thought I was invincible
until the brother of a friend
offered me a lift home.

I was twelve years old. He was nineteen,
on leave from the RAF
where he had received combat training;
a helpful skill when you plan
to drag a minor into the back seat of your car
and rape her.

Squashed beneath him, I heard
a child mewling for
its mother. It took me a while to
notice that the sounds
came from my mouth, since I was focused
on escape from the
pain inflicted by a
hard object like a wet
cricket bat that was
pushing itself toward
my shrinking hymen.

Half a century later,
when I recall that night, my ears
still catch the strain as she whimpers:
"mummy... mum-mummy...."
I feel the slippery blood under my half-built butt,
the fingers that grip,
the drool on my chin
as I taste the metallic flavour of terror.

I'd trusted I was an Amazon,
yet that evening, something split inside me.
A cruel stain seeped out,
spreading across my face,
spelling a single word, invisible
to all but the coldest predators.

"Vulnerable", it said.

I didn't see it
or know I had lost my strength,
neither did I recognise the danger
when the others came for me.

Each time, I imbibed the blame,
nurturing it like it was a ball of glass,
since
if it wasn't my fault, how could I
stop it
from happening again?

Years slid behind me. I let go of the bauble,
displaying it with others for all to see.
I met many sisters who shared their stories with me.
We shouted our truths, our catalogues of abuse,

I watched all the baubles break, smashed
by the singularity of our mission,
freeing us from shame,
giving us the self-esteem
to utter a simple sentence:

"Touch me
and one way or another
I will bury you."

I Never Told Anyone
Kindra M. Austin

I was six years old the first time I ever removed my clothes at a boy's request. His name was ███████, and he had a younger sister called ███████. The three of us played together nearly every day when my family lived on Huggins Road—███████ and ███████ lived with their mother and father directly across the street. It was a hot day. I remember sweating in the dry, prickly grass, staring up at a sky so perfectly blue, I never wanted to look away. ███████ lay on top of me in the backyard of his house; I will never forget the sensation of his flaccid penis smooshed against my labia. Pale skinned and white-blonde, ███████ was naked, too, standing in bright sunbeams—she seemed to glow.

My parents had friends who lived on the other side of Flint. I can't recall their names, but they had a Doberman Pinscher, Angel. The couple had two children, ███████ and ███████, who were both older than me by a good few years. ███████, who frequently liked to pull down his pants and shake his penis in my face, used to show me Playboy magazines that he'd pilfered from his dad.

We moved to Lapeer when I was seven years old. That summer, my mother told my uncle—her baby brother—that he wasn't allowed in the pool with me anymore because she'd caught him with his penis exposed through the slit of his trunks while he and I were swimming together. In elementary school—third grade—a boy named ███████ found a discarded condom on the playground, and told his friends he'd used it on me.

In middle school, there was boy who would always sneak up and stand behind me, then he'd grab my hand and press it into his crotch. By the time I was a freshman, most of my friends had already had sex. When I was fifteen, there was one boy in particular who I crushed hard for, and he liked me, too. His name was ███████. One time, he and his cousin came over to my best friend's house, where I was spending the night, and the four of us went for a walk; we ended up in the woods. I was ultimately left alone with ██████. Holy hell, he was cute. I let him kiss me, and feel me up under my shirt, but over my bra. My eyes welled up when he unzipped his pants, and pressed his erect penis against my pelvis. It was summer, and I was wearing light cloth shorts that were too fucking short. ██████ lay on top of me, forced my legs apart, and humped me quite violently—he didn't penetrate me. I opened his back with my fingernails, but he wouldn't stop. I went for his neck, but he grabbed my wrists and kept on pumping. The skin of my inner thigh had been rubbed so aggressively, it cracked and bled and bruised.

I was married to ███████████████ when he sexually assaulted me. We'd been out drinking. I was incoherently drunk when we arrived home in the middle of the night, but I do remember eating cold pizza, then going to bed in my clothes. I woke up the next day naked from the waist down, bleeding from my anus, and in pain. I remembered he'd told me once that it wasn't illegal to rape your wife in the state of Michigan.

Welcome Home
Kathryn Buonantony

A meeting between the past and present
should transpire soon.
I would hold my thirteen-year-old self
close and whisper, "It's going to be okay."
But, I wonder if she would believe me.
I would let her cry to me and tell
me how she feels like
a rotted peach with its pit pulled out of its body—
she's hollow and has begun to melt into herself
because her body feels like home no longer.

I would explain that she will feel this way
for many years
until she wakes up to a full moon
in a cold sweat
and reclaims herself.
Her name is no longer a slur, but
it is an onrush of empowerment.
It no longer feels foreign to her tongue,
and she does not have to whisper its syllables.
She can howl it at the moon
without fear that he is listening.

I would apologize to myself
for not doing so sooner
because my ten-year-old self was so sure
that she'd change the world.
But, that was before she ever learned of the
harsh realities of beds and broken bones.
Her bed was still a sacred space of refuge
and sweet dreams;
one that could only be thwarted by

the threat of bed bugs.

I would tell my sixteen-year-old self
to not be ashamed of finding solace
sleeping in her mother's bed,
for she can protect you from the monsters
in yours.
At night, you may feel reduced to a child,
but I assure you that will go away in time.
The darkness will not have a hold on you forever.

Of all the things he took from you,
never let your smile fade.
He does not own your teeth,
your lips, your tongue.
You used to bite your cheek until it bled
just to have control,
and now the scars in your mouth are only memories,
fading and pink.

I'd explain to my eighteen-year-old self
that cutting off your hair
was the best decision you would ever make
because one day you would grow a whole
new mane that he will have never touched.
One day you will never be afraid of
flipping it off your shoulder
or letting it blow in the wind.
You changed your life that day
because you were no longer
able to hide.

In retrospect, I'll admit that, yes, I
have let the world taint my once
lofty dreams and maybe I would be

disappointed in myself, but I truly think
I would forgive me, so I could move on
because that ten-year-old is still somewhere
inside me, bright-eyed and hopeful, not
yet the scarred thirteen-year-old
who feels like a ghost in her own
body.

In essence, this is a suicide note, for
I am done with me, the twenty-something
who is anaesthetized to the small voice
of the ten-year-old,
laughing, joking, hoping.
That part of me is on the edge, looking down,
presumably never to be heard from again.
She may be wiser in her own head,
but she still has a lot to learn from
the younger ones.

In essence, this is a birth announcement,
for out of the ashes spring new life:
a ten-year old, care-free, clamoring
toward the future; a bit more bent
than before, but by no means broken.
Yes, a meeting between the past
and present should transpire soon.
A place where the two can blend
harmoniously.
Where tears can be shared
and laughter is heard
until they reconcile their differences,
and can each find her way home
within herself.

I said no and you said yes

Candice Louisa Daquin

I said no and you said yes
The first time was before I can remember
adults do not have dominion over children's souls
but that's what happens when you touch a child and cause her to be
unwhole
the second time was in nursery school so I suppose your foray of my
body had begun
as I emulated what was done
in the back of a toy caravan with my pretend boyfriend and he liked it
a lot
made me feel dirty though I did not know what that meant at the time
seeded a doubt in the core of my person, like a rod of copper slowly
turning green
the third time I lay face down on a dirty carpet and three boys played
marbles across my back
they got the idea from a porno mag their father hadn't hidden very
well
their kid sister watched from the doorway, I told her with my eyes, go
to your room or you will be next
I said no and you said yes
it became as normal as something bad can be, I wanted to see her,
so I had to cross the gauntlet and you were the gatekeeper
nobody believes you when it is easier to disbelieve and go on
thinking respectable people don't lie
you taught me to hate games shows as they were our background
noise and grandma would come in laughing and I'd see the guilt in
her eyes
sacrifice the daughter, sacrifice the child, sweep the dirt underneath
the bruises of generations
at nine I fell in love for the first time with a boy who wiggled above
me but he of all, respected my desire to be unmolested and we hung
upside down from the monkey puzzle tree holding hands

I said no and you said yes
James Brown was your name like the singer, and you didn't take no
for an answer
you climbed my bunk bed and pulled down your pants and if
someone hadn't knocked, would have got your way
I wonder who came after me and if they were saved by the bell?
I said no and you said yes
yes yes yes, you know you want this
no no no, I really don't
but you asked for it, you tempted me, you flirted, you caused me to
have a hard-on, this is YOUR FAULT
I kissed a boy in the garages outside school and it felt dirty and
wrong because it reminded me of what others had done
before I made decisions of my own
I said no and you said yes
I felt guilty about touching myself because of the Jehovah witnesses
and the Mormons and the teacher who stapled my confession
together and said we won't talk of it
when I tried to tell her, this is what happened to me
and you didn't feel guilty about playing Yahtzee and karate on your
father's bed with the nylon sheets and the little bobbles they made
when you made a tent and put your fingers in
and you didn't feel badly when you lied and said you would only
touch and instead you went too far and before I knew you were
pinning me against a table
I said no and you said yes
children who are violated don't always know what's best for them
they are broken and they are scattered and they are stomped on and
they hate how they look when the light is on
but they want to fit in and they want to be normal and sometimes in
trying they get it all wrong
the neighbor told my parents; your little girl is using bad words and
teaching my boys how to curse
and I said fucking hell what does it matter?

182

but it did, it mattered a lot, to stay in the confine of childhood and not grow up

because growing up meant it was real and you had to deal with it and whilst you were a child

nobody believed it could happen anyway so you could pretend it did not

I said no and you said yes

yes yes yes, I know you want to

no no no, I really don't

and my second boyfriend said he wouldn't go too far

but he did and he did and he did

and I ran through the streets holding myself up and I shouted to the trees that had fallen because of the high wind

why do people pretend? because I didn't understand and it was a language impenetrable

but I was not … impenetrable, I was just a place of conquer

I wanted to find a lock and keep myself closed

but they kept battering down the door one after the other

because patterns are sometimes all we have to show for the cycle of abuse

I said no and you said yes

the last time was in a public street

dragged off and soon the roads diminished and the woods were thick

he moved like a silver fish cutting his way into my secrets

I lay staring at the knife

he told me, *I won't cut you if you are nice*

I was very, very nice

no no no

yes yes yes

the policeman said; I have to ask, it's my job, did you want to have sex with this homeless man?

I pulled up my torn skirt and my ripped hose and my shredded blouse and my dismembered bra and my bloody underwear and I said;

if you can even ask that question, you will not recognize justice if it comes

no no no
I said no and you said yes
the last time and the first time and all the rest
when children become girls, become women, become less
than the worth that is owed them
yes yes yes !

"As someone who survived sexual abuse, molestation, and rape, it felt important and meaningful to participate in this anthology. I want others to know they are not alone and they do not have to carry the same shame I once did. I will no longer be silenced. I will find my voice again and again. It is my hope that someone else may find the strength to turn a silent prayer into a whisper - into a ferocious roar as they claim the words they need to speak their truth. This is how we heal: one person, one voice, one story, and one poem at a time."

Mary A. Rogers Glowczwskie

Vignettes Of Violation

HLR

1.
I may be crazy, lonely, drunk
I may wear a smile caked in red paint
I may not wear a wedding ring
I may be wearing a shirt that shrunk in the wash
I may politely respond to your small-talk
I may accept or decline your offer to buy me a drink
I may tell you my real name
I may give you a fake phone number
I may be wearing my highest heels
I may listen to your life story
I may genuinely like you, strange man;
but when you tried to kiss me
and I pushed you away and said,
"No, what are you doing?! Get off me!"
none of the above factors were invitations
for you to try again,
    with force,
        with hands,
            with teeth,
                with malice,
                    with black eyes,
                        with whisky breath,
                          with entitlement.

2.
It crushes me to think how many times in my short life
I've had to utter these words to a man:
So what, you bought me drink? I owe you *nothing*.

3.
I was outside a famous London pub, two days after Christmas,
Lugging on a cigarette in the bitter cold.

185

A man approached me and asked to borrow my lighter.
I handed it over without saying a word.
He put it in the front pocket of his jeans.
I asked for it back, thinking he'd made a genuine error.
He said I can get it back after I've had a drink and a dance with him.
He tapped his pocket, near his crotch.
His smile made my skin crawl.
"Keep it," I said, and ran inside.
I watched him: he was pestering other single women for lighters.
Several weeks later I was reading a newspaper.
Printed on page 8 was a CCTV image taken outside the pub,
On that night, at that time, when I was there,
My boyfriend and I sitting in the window.
The man loitering outside.
That hair, that jacket, those trainers.
They were appealing for information about him.
15 minutes after that image was captured,
He raped a girl down the side street.
It could've been me.
She was my age.
It should've been me.
I read the article and threw up.
It could've been me.
I felt such guilt.
It should've been me.
If I'd spoken to him for a minute longer,
If I'd fought him for my lighter,
If I'd caused a scene,
If I'd done something, anything differently,
That girl and life as she knew it wouldn't have changed forever.
It was almost me.
It was almost me too.

4.

When I was 8 years old, a family friend taught me one of the most valuable lessons a girl could ever learn. I remember him bringing his scarred, tattooed face down next to mine and saying in a hushed voice, "If ever a man makes you feel uncomfortable or scared or in danger in any way, what you've got to do is kick him in the bollocks as hard and fast as you can. If you do it right, you can incapacitate a man, and then you run. Got it?" This advice has saved me in more situations that I'd care to admit, although I must mention one incident in which this advice served me particularly well, a decade after I had first taken it on board. That same family friend was making me feel uncomfortable and scared and in danger and found himself on the receiving end of his own advice. I try to avoid violence where possible, but the sensation of his testes against the force of my knee, seeing him buckle to the ground, moaning, wearing a face of sheer agony and eyes full of apology and tears, was worth the damage. He never touched me again.

5.

When did it become normal?
Was it when I was a child and saw a man pleasuring himself
on a park bench?
Was it when that man flashed his genitals at us
at the gates of our all girls' school?
Was it when I was eating cherries at the bus stop
and a stranger asked me what else I could do with my tongue?
Was it when we were kids dressing as adults, showing skin,
trying desperately hard to look old enough to get served in a pub?
Was it when you flashed your underage breasts at the shopkeeper
to get him to sell you cigarettes?
Was it when that guy put his hands down my tights in a busy shop
and told me not to scream or make scene?
Was it when I ate a banana in public
and a stranger called me a filthy slut?
Was it when my friend's boyfriend grabbed my wrist

and shoved my hand down his trousers?
Was it when we were teenagers and were delighted when a passing white van man
beeped his horn at us because we thought it meant we were attractive?
Was it when we began calling the unsolicited attention of strange men
"Confirmation" because we believed their leers confirmed that we looked good?
Was it when I woke up in an unfamiliar room with my jeans around my knees,
bruises between my thighs and a man taking photographs?
Was it when he put his face in my breasts and I didn't do anything because he was old and drunk and has a granddaughter my age?
Was it the first time someone pinched my bum? The 24th time? The 76th time?
Was it when he followed me into the Ladies toilets, pushed me into a cubicle,
and locked the door behind us?
Was it when I said "No" over 100 times and cried and pushed him away
and he still carried on, telling me that I loved it?
Was it when we went to the police station to report a sexual assault and the female police officer told us to wear less make-up?
Was it when we went to a teacher to report a sexual assault and he said it's our fault for being so pretty?
Was it when the sexual health nurse told us it's our fault if we have an alcoholic drink and get assaulted because we were asking for it?
Was it when I only realised very recently that I am a victim, because I've never felt like one or been treated like one because all my life I thought
that getting flashed and groped and taken advantage of and exploited and manipulated
and being frightened and ashamed and disgusted and embarrassed

188

was NORMAL?
I don't feel like a victim, and while that is a blessing, it is also part of the problem.

"I have been hushed, and shushed, and pinned down my entire life. Being published in this anthology has made me feel like a lion with the most ferocious roar. I have never felt so powerful. "

Carrie Weis

#MeToo
Lesléa Newman

piano teacher sitting beside me on the bench sliding his hand
beneath my behind;

dentist reclining my chair all the way back and resting his tools on my
chest;

friend of my father's pulling me onto his lap and promising to make
me a star;

mail carrier walking behind me calling, "I wish that swing was in my
back yard;"

man driving by in blue car yelling, "Nice tits;"

man driving by in white car yelling, "Hey, shine those headlights over
here;"

man on subway rubbing up against me;

man on subway showing me his dick;

man on subway doing a manspread and pressing his thigh against
mine;

man in mostly empty movie theatre sitting next to me, then changing
his seat when I changed my seat five times until I finally left;

man standing next to his parked truck with his dick in his hand calling
to me, "Wanna play with it, baby?"

man in toy store touching himself while holding Betsy Wetsy and
smiling at me;

man in elevator extending his business card saying, "You're very
beautiful. Give me a call;"

mentor at poetry retreat saying, "Forget your poetry. Let's talk about
your beautiful eyes;"

man sitting beside me on airplane calling me a bitch because I
declined the drink he offered to buy me;

man sitting beside me on airplane calling me a bitch because after
ten minutes of small talk I said I had work to do and needed quiet;

man at encounter group introductory meeting squeezing my breasts
during a trust exercise when I was blindfolded then bragging about it
afterwards;

man riding by on bike grabbing my breasts and then pedaling away;
man leaving love notes in my mailbox telling me we were meant to
be together and throwing pebbles at my window at 3:00 a.m.;
cop responding to my call saying, "What's the matter? He only wants
to get to know you;"
man walking by me at 2:00 in the afternoon saying, "Wanna fuck?"
boss making me try on all the clothes in the boutique where I worked
and demanding that I stand still while he adjusted them on my body;
customer staring at my breasts for more than ten minutes without
saying a word knowing I was alone in the store and couldn't leave
my cash register;
housemate's boyfriend crawling into bed with me after housemate
left for work;
gay man telling me, "If I was straight, I would fuck you;"
poetry teacher saying, "Oh, you're a feminist? I know how to fix that;"
I will long remember each and every one of you
as surely as each and every one of you has long forgotten me

The Scars of a Good Girl
Jack Neece

I was so small in that bed every night. He touched me and told me this is what good Daddies do. He told me that is friends just wanted to show me a good time, and I should be grateful for the attention. He told me that I was to be a good girl. He taught me what it meant to be a girl in this world. He taught me that I was merely a piece of a human, the only piece that mattered when you're a girl. His hands were in every moment of my life as I grew. His hands were in my head when my friend and her boyfriend went dancing giddily into the bedroom and winked as they left me on the couch with the stranger and his lustful gaze. My father's hands reached down my throat and silenced me when this stranger looked at me, licked his lips and said, "This is going to happen one way or the other." My father smiled in my head as I was a good girl and let him slide inside me because that is what good girls do. I didn't want to get raped and beaten so I settled for just the rape. I could feel that smile slide around my body with every sexual experience. I could never wash it off or cut it away from me, but God how I tried. I could feel my father's hands and the imprints they left on my mind. It's visual for me ya know? When my father reached inside me and scooped out my innocence, he took with him a piece of my soul. He took my "No" from me. It eventually wasn't rape anymore right? I didn't fight anymore so I liked it right? I was a good girl now right? I was fulfilling my destiny as a woman that was "nothing more than a wet hole in a mattress", right Daddy? I was a good girl, right Daddy? He forced his way inside me and made me his. This man eviscerated a child and I still hear his words every time a man yells obscenities at me. "Hey!! Nice tits!! Can I get your number!? Hey! Hey!?! I'm talking to you!! BITCH!!! You should say Thank You. That just means you're pretty and valuable. You should be grateful that the boys like you." I feel like screaming. I want to tear at the flesh of every person that touched me. I want to fight now for the little girl that couldn't. I want to go back into those moments when it was his face laid over every man that didn't have my permission and take my no back. I want to tell them all that my body is mine. I want to scream that they don't have my permission. I want to rage and claw at the fabric of a society that allows the systematic destruction of its women. I want to fight for every little girl lying in her bed being touched by the devil. I actually did take the devil to court. I actually did "win". Thank God Daddy was so violent. Thank God the scars he left could still be seen and documented by credible doctors. Thank God the medical evidence was on my side. This is what I was told. The words of a child wasn't enough. I had to be raped all over again in the court room. "What positions did the defendant put you in?" "Well what time of year was it?" "What kind of clothing did you have on?" "Surely you got this idea from all of the pornography you watch." The first time I testified I was 11. My father's attorney argued that I was a violent masturbator and merely seeking attention. Again, I was 11. I mentioned my father's friends that had raped me to my attorney. I was told not to bring it up in court. It would only dilute our case and pull focus from my father. The system would never convict multiple men of "one crime". Yeah, this was my legal advice from my attorneys. My father did ten years for taking my mind, my soul, and my virginity. Ten years later he was out of his cage. I am 39, I will let you know when I get out of mine. I have men in my life now that scare me. My father's hands still slither around my throat when they get too close. I will never be free of the things that man did to me, the things his friends did to me. Survival now is a double edged sword. I am stronger but not because of him. I am stronger in spite of him. I am a woman growing in a society of broken and battered women. We are quiet because we are told we should be. We accept the things done because, well, boys will be boys. We are shoved into the dirt and made to eat our words every day. I have been told rape is a a relative term. I mean eventually it couldn't have been that bad, it's not like I was a virgin every time. I shudder at the fact that these are all things that have been said to me. The non-issue that rape is for such a huge portion of our society is baffling to me. How is it not seen as an evil and heinous act to enter another humans body against their will? It seems simple to me. I am sure it seems simple to every person that has ever been raped. I am sure this is the only thing simple about it.

"For too long we women have shed silent tears, made our sufferings our shroud to escape the tyrannies and taboos. I feel this is the right time in the history for women to resurrect their lost voices and finally narrate the horrors of their tales."

Tanya Shukla

Ossuary
Sabrina Escorcio

She attempts to stand
upon uneven ground
atop a broken earth divide,
awkwardly balancing
between woman and child

Fissures of inheritance
the infectious bane
of her own existence,
formed beneath calloused soles
of sister, mother, grandmother

Charms contained within
the broken locket placed
delicate around her neck;
sacred curse of ancestry adorned,
yet blessed by envious men

Gaping hole expectations
inscribed in faint palm lines
anticipate a descent from innocence,
as brute, unforgiving hands voyage
forging reckless trespass

They emerge in procession
seeking temporary resolve
within the brimstone depths of
her fractured heart pedestal; built
by brother, father , grandfather

Instinctively she continues
heart blind and bound

planting seeds of trust, inside
the empty moral vessel
of a nutrient void society

Bedded upon a shroud
of ivory bridal linens,
virgin hope buried in white
between quivering legs; her
ever consuming crimson tide

She who didn't resemble me
Candice Louisa Daquin

The day I was raped and ruined and rebuilt and lived and died and
survived
I hadn't yet been born
it happened instead to my mother
she who didn't resemble me
it happened to the woman my father took after my mother left
she who didn't resemble me
it happened to my cousin who wouldn't have been my cousin
if not for terrible deeds and women who refused to be quenched
we slept
in a state of not yet existing
in a time when there was no mouthpiece to whisper into
my mother's father he is coming into her room at night, he is taking
off
his clothes and lying next to her and I do not like how he looks
when the moon catches his wolfish mouth and what he does with
his little finger
I go back in time to speak to my mother
but her chest is pressed to the wall of her small room
she does not say anything to me, she is still becoming
she is not going to reform now that he broke her
she is going to be shards and borders and lines and shattered
and look more beautiful for it and survive more because of it
and the only part that will not
thrive
will be her instinct to love me
which was crushed by him before I ever
existed
I go into the next room
my step mother who was my world when I was 11
is also a little girl
she has been taken by the authorities

to a children's home and cries herself to sleep
because as much as she could not understand
why her father touched her in her mother's bed
after she died
she was so glad someone loved her
and now that love has gone
I see above her head
the twists and turns, the knife and cuts of misunderstanding and shame
love can be so easily perverted
children do not understand, but they grow into their roles
as my step mother grew into alternately hating me and loving me
Ihateyoulloveyoulhateyoulloveyou
I read about the link between sexual abuse and borderline personality disorder
in my psychology class
that was after, my grandfather won a triple crown
for abusing three generations
(I was the last)
(fuck him I was the last!)
that was before
I was raped by a man on the run for strangling
who left me bleeding on the street
(this was before I knew much of my dear adopted country)
(I found out soon enough)
the three of us
play with our hair
it is shorn by exhaustion and stands up in tufts
rebuking the desire to give up
if these decisions to abuse had not been made
maybe my mom would have stayed
maybe I'd never have met my step mom
maybe I would be a mother myself
these damaging actions
changed the trajectory of three women

through the ages, those who are raped in battles that are not their
battles
raped in marriages where they have no rights
raped at parties and told if you hadn't been asking for it
raped at home where you are supposed to be safe
they don't stop
and even with terrible scars
that add to the surfeit of pain
they endure
sometimes I think I love them more
because of their imperfection and the
survival in their eyes

Stay
Anonymous

Unsafe people tell you, *At least if you wrote fiction, you'd have a
   chance to make some money.*
Unsafe people imply, *Look, let's talk, or I'm going to make up shit
   about you.*
Unsafe people say you don't have enough evidence.
Unsafe people say, *I know people,* and drop their names drip by drip.
Unsafe people riffle through your desk drawers for evidence.
Unsafe people bide their time, leaving you at the elevator shaft at the
   perfect time. They pray you plunge down, not rise up.
Unsafe people say they're proud to know you.
Unsafe people won't greet you at their doors.
Unsafe people get up from behind their desks and back you up to the
   door.
Unsafe people say they can make you.
Unsafe people ask what makes you high.
Unsafe people circle around you after the accident and smirk.
Unsafe people keep asking you how you're doing after you say, *Fine*.
Unsafe people find you alone.
Unsafe people sneak up on you from behind.
Unsafe people can get you readings, a spot on a panel, a grant.
Unsafe people look up your skirt, use elevator eyes.
Unsafe people hack and hack and hack.
Unsafe people flatter you too much.
Unsafe people say, *You have so much empathy.*
Unsafe people praise everyone else to you.
Unsafe people tell everyone you're a liar.
Unsafe people say, *I didn't see it,* but they did see it.
Unsafe people corner your responses in passing--they won't look at
   you/they won't let you not look at them.
Unsafe people have armies of unsafe people, their people, spying,
   gossiping, inventing.
Unsafe people disappear when you win an award.

Unsafe people have minimal time, they have to go, they have too
  many unsafe people to see, to text, to sleep with.
Unsafe people use their melodic voices.
Unsafe people stay cool.
Unsafe people collect shoelaces and tie them to their bedsteads.
Unsafe people hoover you after you've left.
Unsafe people enter your house when you aren't there and move
  things around.
Unsafe people have all the time in the world when you spill your
  secrets, your voice cracking open. They love that. They eat
  it up and spew it out.
Unsafe people imagine you surrounded by shabby hotel walls, a
  plastic razor hovering over your arm's vein.
You can hear unsafe people sigh when you don't press the razor
  down, as you get out of the door, when a safe person walks
  over, when you, gazelle beauty, speed away, stay safe,
    stay.

Telling stories
Elizabeth Beaver

I loved stories,
To hear,
To tell,
Of dreams,
And dragons,
I told my cousin about a haunted house,
She cried,
Then I had to tell it again,
To my angry father,
Who admitted,
It was quite convincing.
I told my brother,
that the mountains were dragons,
That had laid down for a long sleep,
And still lay silently waiting.
I told my mother
Of lovers reaching for each other,
Across a gap with no bridge,
She asked how I a child could know of love,
And I shrugged,
How could I not know?
I'd read all of the stories.
The stories were mine,
The ones I made and the ones I'd found.
The stories were me,
Intertwined around my being.
I loved stories,
I'd paint them out,
A girl who ran with wolves,
A song that the sun and moon sang to each other,
And everyone loved my stories,
Little girl,

Big imagination,
But when I told them why I was afraid to sleep,
Why I'd hide in the closet at night,
No one believed,
Maybe I blamed myself,
Maybe I blamed the stories,
Because one by one,
the stories went away.

When I Told
Cynthia L Bryant

When I told my mother
    she said
 "Do you feel guilty?"

When I told my aunt
    she said
"I'm not surprised."

When she told her husband
    he said
"I wish you hadn't told me."

When I told my uncle
    he said
"Gee that's too bad, but that was a long time ago."

When he told his wife
    she said
"Too bad something wasn't said while he was living,
so he could have defended himself."

When I told my cousin
    she said
"There was a rumor of it in our mothers' family."

When I told my husband
    my father had sexually abused me throughout my childhood
He held me while I cried.

Why I Stayed Silent
Nicholas Gagnier

There seems to
be
some
confusion why I didn't tell you
like you were a friend or
family member or
a fucking
snowflake in
December, entitled to the life force of my greatest omission.

You ask
why I stayed
silent about whom I kissed or who touched me without
permission; why I was conditioned
to mistrust
every
last one of you intolerable cunts, who
may have given me life but never love, who
sat back and judged
and then
wanted to give my
evolution a numbered score.

Now I'm zero to ten
because counting's a chore and I just want to
blow the
roof off
inside a split second.

You ask why
I didn't tell you- the
answer is so violent,

you
really don't need to know.

"When I get up to read these poems I imagine throwing a life vest out to listeners. Its amazing when one or two people come up after, touch my arm and tell me a bit of their story. Bravely telling our truth can inspire someone to grab that life vest."

Rachael Ikins

Desecrated
Tiffany K. Elliot

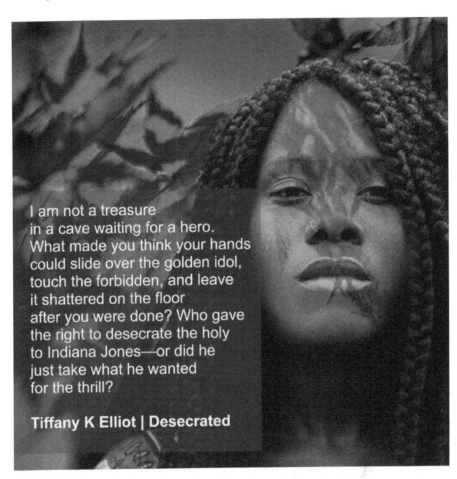

I am not a treasure
in a cave waiting for a hero.
What made you think your hands
could slide over the golden idol,
touch the forbidden, and leave
it shattered on the floor
after you were done? Who gave
the right to desecrate the holy
to Indiana Jones—or did he
just take what he wanted
for the thrill?

Tiffany K Elliot | Desecrated

The Day the Light Faded
Ashley Jane

you stare,
enamored,
watching her every move,
determined to leave your name
tattooed beneath her skin

you call her an alchemist,
a vixen, enchantress, witch
she is none of those things

just a girl
who once looked at life
through bright eyes

just the ghost of a girl
who will never forget
your face,
      voice,
      smell,
      touch,
      the day the light faded
      from the sky

but do not count her out just yet
one day
she'll remember how to shine
one day
she'll become the sun

Brute
Eric Syrdal

This is something I need to write
while the fire of anger is in my heart
In these later years of my life
I have learned to let go of anger
more quickly
so what is left of my heart doesn't become
blackened and bitter
But I must say this
You disgust me
You have my complete contempt
and that is not an easy thing to do
I have a forgiving heart
I strive to understand
to accept
to empathize
I cannot do this with you
You confound me to no end
I am continuously embarrassed and confused
by your actions
You cannot comprehend how much
rage fills my heart when I think of you
what you do
what you consider amusement
is a sick and twisted malady
which is incurable in the likes of you
what gives you the right
to approach her?
what broken logic
do you mutter to yourself
in the throes of your indecent behavior
you can't be content
with all the warnings we are given as children

you can't be satisfied
that a butterfly perched upon your finger
You can not marvel at her beauty
with eye-watering wonder
You can not sit in peace
as she shows you her gorgeous colors
close your eyes and feel
the tingle in your soul at her delicate touch
upon your skin
sigh out loud
at the pride swelling in your heart
that she chose you
as a place to rest from her weary flight
You had to touch her wings
Your alpha-bullshit
convinced you that you could do such a thing
and she would be fine
and so with slobbering tongue and whining like a beast in heat
intent on humping the furniture
you repeatedly let your primitive hind-brain
type out a string of tripe to her
always on a private channel
because your coward nature doesn't let you make advances in the
light
where men such as I
could see
and oh how I wish you would give me the chance to see
You inspire me to violence
because you make me physically ill
Your alpha-animal-fuckery makes me want to
give in to my primal side too
and thrash you within an inch of your life
So of that you can be proud...you drag me kicking and screaming to
your level
I hate you for it

You can't walk past a beautiful flower
without putting your filthy hands around the stem
and yanking her from the earth?
On this massive battlefield that we all share
you can't celebrate her strength and power
without hooking a finger behind her breastplate to see
what's underneath?
How dare you, you wretched filthy piece of trash.....
In this war we all fight
how good does it feel to protect her flank?
take one more worry off her mind
that she can feel confident you are an ally
You will never know
what it feels like to put your back against hers
and devote all of your willpower to the forces in front of you
never worrying that something may attack from behind
I enjoy
so much
lying on the ground
next to their fire and watching the beautiful shapes
amid their crackling flames
They warm what is left of my soul and you have no idea the battle
that I fight to keep it every day
and you are putting them out
these wonderful bonfires of strength and beauty
sensual and romantic
hard edged and joyful
you are snuffing them out one by one
and I hate you for it
with every shame-laden-panic-attack-inducing
unwanted advance
you remove more and more of them from my universe
and I am tired of it
So very tired

They owe you nothing
and that is all you will ever be

"Too many women have had the voice inside them strangled and silenced. If I can find the strength to speak out, and am offered the chance to have my voice amplified, it's my duty to stand up for those who cannot. I hear you. I believe you. I see you. I am you. #METOO"

Grace Alexander

Tom at the Bar
Carla Schwartz

He hovers at the bar
in the middle, on the outside
his oily straight hair
lends rake to his silhouette
as he reigns with his bottle
from between the seated.

He feigns credibility
in his suit jacket.
With half an ear,
he listens to the music.
The bar is crowded with couples
so he has no one to talk to
until he notices me,
a vagina with a pretty face,
standing behind a tall table,
listening intently, writing.

How many beers did it take
to dream up his opener?
*Are you stealing
her songs?*
Quite a few
in not too long.

Thief of Dreams
Jay Long

Hey there little boy
Sitting in your high chair
With an entitled grin
and societal exception
You coward
You thief of dreams
Remember her name
Remember her face
She is a survivor
full of strength and dignity
So glad Daddy could hold your hand
and beg for your mercy with the deep pockets of privilege
Lust driven enough to take what you want
Not man enough to face the fire
But you will
The gates of hell
will welcome you home one day
How does it feel
to rip out someone's soul
and keep your freedom
When there's no acquittal from her pain
and no escaping the life sentence
your "20 minutes of action" handed down

Shadows
Ramansuresh

Shadows
creepy, crawly
stalking pavements
a graffiti of reeking
scarlet spittles of freaks
Beware woman
your steel of nerves
your spiky nails
peel out the skins

shadows
scabby, queasy
slimy fins sneaking on board
brutes rubbing skins
Beware woman
Your armour of verve
your ivory fangs
cut off those fins

Shadows
foxy, crafty
in the darkness of homes
hooded eyes and hearts
of toxic kinships
Beware woman
Your voice of valor
Your tough palates
disgrace those liars

Scars of Wonder
Michelle Schaper

I wonder what it's like
to be able to dance
out in public without
being called a tramp

I wonder what it's like
to walk alone
without holding tight
onto keys and a phone

I wonder what it's like
to have the windows open wide
without fearing someone lurking
from just outside

I wonder what it's like
to wear minimal clothing when it's hot
or drink out till I'm drunk
take more than one shot

I wonder what it's like
to wait in my car, not lock the door
but mostly I wonder why no one asks
what my rapists wore.

Running Home
Kristiana Reed

I'm walking home
holding my house key
pointing down, between
two fingers.
A weapon

because the sun has set
the street lamps are on
and I'm a twenty four
year old woman.
I'm wearing boots
jeans and a hoodie
but wonder if the flesh
on my palms
will be cause for a judge
to say she was showing
too much skin.
When he ponders

the trauma of a woman
undone; her rage
and her no
not enough. She
should have done more,
she should have worn more,
she should have run faster,
she should have looked
behind her more,
she should

have considered
the temptation

of the breath on her lips,
in her lungs and in her blood
more.

I'm running home -
praying there won't
be a monster waiting for me
in the darkness

behind my closed
front door.

Assaulted
Marcia J. Weber

you were pushed from behind

I heard in the breathless notch
in your measured words
that catch
in your voice
the tremulous quaver
in your understated stand

I have felt those hands
(haven't we all)
one knife-wielding
- in word or deed –
while the other lays claim
with eyes or clammy paws
to my plush backside

you are the embodiment
of cultured terror apparent
the carbon dated anguish
etched on your skin
your pain quivers
on articulated tips
of your educated tongue

I jump sky high
elbow cocked in self- defense
it fades yet never ebbs
that stretched rubber band
that inhabits cells
twangs unbidden

and we sproing!

he tantrums
spews vile rhetoric
wields his power
            his privilege
in ways she would burn
at stake
would she dare give voice
            were she to cry crocodile
            her ovaries would fry
                    ahhh those tantrums
                    we choke down
                    swallow hot with rancid bile
                    those that would label
                    rabid bitch
                    raving *psycho*

because well behaved women
may bare our ankles
            here in 2018
            shoulders even (Oh my!)
                    but we step NOT
                    upon the tender toes
                    of fragile male privilege
under pain of recompense

Assault, Ad Nauseum
Marcia J. Weber

the rape, ironically
was only the beginning
of the assaults

those penetrating moments
intoxication blurred
splattered a visceral montage
burned into retina
tattooed onto neurons
imprinted, lacerating, into cell fibers
they lurk, Lochness monsters
beneath the surface
drag her
gulping mouthfuls of horror
suffocating
in the undertow
now and then

the soundtrack
needle on the record
needle on the record
needle on the record
is the aftermath

the boyfriend
who responds to her question
(early morning shocked and hungover)
"Is it rape if you're too drunk to make them stop?"
with "just go to work" instructions
(ever the worker bee, she showers,
goes to work, where the assailant awaits)
followed, in subsequent days

with an impossible dichotomy
endorse retribution
or acknowledge consent
relationship ends
self-doubt persists

the girlfriends
evening following
whose helpful solution
to repeated blurting
of her reality
is well-schooled
good girl avoidance
"let's go get drunk"
as her torment
slices too close to the bone
of experiences
they pretended away

the nurse
emergency room jaded
steri-stripped of empathy
whose face banged the gavel
when indoctrinated Catholicism
spoke in her voice
refusing morning after pills

the detective
whose investigative strategies
consisted of assigning blame
to wayward vaginas
that frighten him for his daughter
(her age, he emphasizes)
despite his assiduous
applications of guilted

chastity belts
while enshrining the statement
"consensual"
of the other

the prosecutor
(months delayed,
read persistent self-advocacy)
who dropped preparation
in favor of lunch
blindsided her
before the grand jury
referencing nonexistent conversation
automatic pilot kicks in
appeasing, she nods assent
another helpful helper noted

forever fuming
her voicelessness
in the aftermath

225

How many women does it take?
Candice Louisa Daquin

It was raining the day the movers truck pulled up
piling furniture into the back, exposed to wet streets
everything dirty and unfamiliar
when you take your safety out of its box
unlatch your secrets, expose the insides of a locket
sticky mouths seek to further that exposure
until nothing of your peace remains
but the belly of your secrets on display
as if you were sitting in class without underwear
as if the abuse etched in your soul were a t-shirt
as if his fingers weren't in the dark but had been
dipped in luminescent paint and everywhere they went
left their grimy imprint / yet you think
this horror may have been the very best thing
as wretched as exposure may taste, at least it wouldn't be a case of
disbelief
how many women does it take?
for one person to not hesitate
how many must say;
he did this / that happened / we are not okay
because of this / why do I have to prove / with gore
and soiled soul / the truth / why isn't it sufficient that I say
why
did he lay a hand on me?
how many women does it take?
a juror in the Bill Cosby case disclosed the reason for his guilty
verdict;
"I believed he was guilty because he said he had drugged girls,
hearing it from the horse's mouth got my vote"
are we bidding on a horse? Did you check the inside of her mouth?
what of the SIXTY women who spoke?

their voices do not warrant proof? Were people just speaking words?
To deaf sign posts stating;
move on / get over it / don't make a fuss / why should we believe
you?
one person has lied before / you must be lying / that's our automatic
default
what hope then
for one girl?
one single soul, violated in the dark
of a house when all is moved out
and she is left inside a shell, within a shell
the echoes of trucks taking memories
somewhere else
how many women does it take?
to be heard.

The Miss Trial
Crystal Kinistino

In thirty years he will have forgotten you, but the memory of him
remains methylated in your DNA, and blood does not betray in a
court of law. In thirty years that feeling will thaw and become raw
when you see the likes of Brett Kavanaugh take the stand, only then
will they understand the gravity of what holds us down as women
and them up as men. As all the world took a stand against the man in
the robe, our sisters were willing to throw their lives under the bus for
us, and for the first time in history, even men took to the streets and
contested for the girls who were molested, while Dr. Ford invested
her reputation to speak the truth. You watched as the girl in you died
and though you couldn't revive her, you went on to become a
survivor. The laughter of their leader added salt to the wounds of
everyone who had been abused. The message was clear, speak and
lose your dignity, whilst another man's life was held in supreme
honour and civility. Mothers held their daughters, as the ones in
cages were spared the rage of those so-called victimized men, yet
for the ones deemed savages there was another plan, because you
must understand, in a country where no privileged white man is truly
legal, speaking the truth can be lethal. So while we go on living like
warriors with the past coded deep in our cell methylation, we mustn't
forget what that tells of this Nation, we must fight injustice as long as
Brett sits on that throne, for though they may have sworn him in, we
never condoned, because somewhere in our bodies lies a seed, and
no matter how deep they try to bury it with violence, it comes back
like a weed which they will never be able to silence.

Women Learn
Sabrina Escorcio

As an infant, I learned
a smile to a stranger,
did not always bring
kindness in return.

As a child, I learned
the softness of my skin,
mirrored the weakness
I carried within.

As a girl, I learned
the curve of my thighs
and plumpness of my breasts,
were not a blessing,
but a curse, disguised.

As a woman, I know
I am merely prey,
this, the thorn I carry
every day.

Soul Rape
Marcia J. Weber

naked and shackled
she is penned to the page

she clutches tattered
vestiges of dignity
shredded
she fails to cover herself
or fend off
the vicious stripping
of her privacy

with each heinous
thrust of pointed nibs
they anoint themselves
absolved of depravity
in her proclaimed guilt

"Isn't it true
you were wearing
your naivete
cut down to there?"
they berate her
in rhythmic assaults

"we know you
strutted around in
your belief
in human goodness"
they pound into her
bruised and battered

"we have pictures

of your giving nature
skin-tight, slit
to the moon"
they leer, animalistic
hiss and sneer

"we have witnesses
who will testify
you trusted
much too loosely
whore"
they exhaust themselves
emptying poison
into her limp vessel

as with all
who become their prey
she falls silent
convinced any fight
provokes further violations

she closes her mind
shutters shattered psyche
while they chuckle
grin in self-congratulation
wiping themselves off
after the rape
of her soul

Stone Angel
Christine E. Ray

I envision myself
alabaster
hard
cold
smooth
immune
to laser gaze
of strangers
that undress me
objectify me
judge me
reduce me
to curves
to openings
they were never invited
to explore
two X chromosomes
sentence me
to a lifetime of eyes
that look
but do not see
words uttered about my body
like a horse being sold
at market
that scratch and burn
like fingernails on the chalkboard
of my psyche
from mouths
that I fantasize sewing shut
with thick black thread
licking the blood dripping
down their vulnerable bare chests

while I undress them callously
with my acid eyes
judge their assets appraisingly
studs for breeding
and observe that they would be
much handsomer
if they smiled more
if I was not
alabaster

Manguage, or, The Art of Being Perpetually Misunderstood

Rebecca Cairns

Manguage is lip reading in a broken mirror,
Piecing together refractured syllables
And twisted sounds in a puzzle
With no finished picture.
Manguage is not for my benefit.
Mente et manu was my school mantra:
With mind and hand. Understand,
Man did not always mean male
But we've altered words that meant
'To do' and 'to think'
To equate with having balls.

Manguage is the gun preloaded with my epitaph:
I have my finger on the trigger but
Manguage is the catch.
Manguage could call me a bachelor
But it chooses spinster instead.
Manguage could call me a player,
But brands slag across my forehead.
Manguage could call me a stud,
But only a slut will spread her legs.
Manguage uses cunt as the punchline,
Pussy at the butt of every joke,
Manguage has yoked bad connotations
To every name you have for me.
So when someone calls you weak
Or wet, a sissy or douche, a nancy or jessie
When they call you a big girl's blouse
You're hurt because you've been taught
That to be feminine sucks.
My gender is the stick used to beat us all;

Manguage is the muscle that swings it.
Manguage makes sure that when I run like a girl
Or punch like a girl, or win like a girl,
You still understand that men rule the world.

Manguage is giving me a voice with a bridle:
Tongue binds that trap my lines,
Breaks my rhythm, forces rhyme
Chokes me on my protest cries.
Manguage is the sound of centuries,
Stories of histories reported by the victor,
His voice frames my narratives,
Metaphors and allegories, instructional geographies
Of how to be a woman according to man.
I pen my thoughts in biased tongues
Our nouns and verbs and adjectives
Are all designed for different minds.
Sometimes I create new words, I find
The vocabulary provided unrefined.
But what can't define my feelings still defines me.
These are not my words, but they dictate who I can be
What I can do, the doors that open and close
The paths which I can choose,
Or not.
I'm strangled by this mangled language;
I'm forced to bite my tongue.

Manguage is every feeling being *fernweh*,
A thought that can't be contained
In the linguistic limits you've given me.
Manguage means my emotions are a foreign concept
That takes an extra minute to explain.
Manguage is why I ask you to be precise,
Manguage is why I spend hours arguing with men
Over definitions and semantics:

They think verbal sparring is romantic
But I'm exhausted,
Because manguage is tirelessly translating
What you say versus what you mean:
I'm listening for the inbetween, reading
The way you said it, not what you said,
Deciphering your consonants and vowels
Fighting a constant battle in my head
To express myself,
Express anything at all.
I want words that don't undermine my existence
Don't simplify my feelings, don't qualify being quelled.
If I had a language that served me
The way women have served you for centuries
I'd wrap my wrath in raps and give you hell.

Manguage is the white noise between radio play
The static energy that drowns the silence, fills the void,
So you don't notice the lack, the drought.
Manguage tells us all about the, "He said, she said"
Like there are two sides to any story;
Like her lines aren't drafted from the loose change
Of his hundred dollar bill.
My two-cents means nothing
When it's measured up against his linguistic wealth,
When I preface my speeches with self-deprecating:
"I think, if I could, just a thought, I'm probably wrong, but...."
And I can hear my dad now, telling me
He didn't bring me up this way, he taught me
Everything he knows and gave me his voice
So I could be heard above the noise:
He doesn't know that when my mouth opens
And his words come out, I'm bossy, not the boss.
Manguage is the one class I will never pass,
The test I will always fail.

Manguage is the tongue I can never master,
Because I will always be its mistress.

Manguage is turning up the volume with the mute button on;
It's listening to the lyrics only half way through the song.
Manguage is why we rely on
Tones and lips and eyes,
It's why I second guess your meaning, read between the lines
It's why I take my time to say what I mean,
It's why I cry when you say you hear me, and you don't.
It's why I cry, because sometimes there are no words,
No lines,
No metaphors.
Manguage is why sometimes I say nothing at all.

The crime is how we feel about ourselves
Candice Louisa Daquin

Did it change me?
That's the question I'm asked the most
It seems irrelevant compared to
What was it like thinking you'd contracted HIV?
When you found out he had AIDS and still raped?
What did it feel like to know he was a murderer and
If they hadn't interrupted his fingers may have
Squeezed and choked you too
As it was, he whispered, *I like your cunt a lot*
You're the first foreign bitch I've fucked
Nobody asks the right questions
You pretend it's okay to be talking about it
As if it were a small thing, a thing of sense
How can words, shape feelings or describe cries?
What has changed and died, what has not existed
Never was I so grateful to take the morning after pill
Never was I so horrified to hear the policeman say;
Maybe as a lesbian you got tired of being with women and you went
out that day in your demure outfit and wanted a homeless man with
serial rape and murder hanging over his unwashed head to
Scoop you up and take you drugged to a filthy warehouse
Where moving aside your sanitary towel he dove into your menstrual
blood
And sucked on your breasts with sharp yellow teeth
While you watched the rats and felt nails in your back and his fingers
around your throat
Where afterward you could not walk, so you dragged yourself on
your belly
And even then, cars drive past
Better questions are:
What did it feel like …
Waiting for pregnancy tests

Waiting for the results of STD panels
Sitting in a room whilst they decide if you qualify for treatment
Because student insurance is all used up
Taking HIV prophylactic retrovirals
Puking up your empty stomach
No family coming
Alone in your second month in America
Hearing his southern accent murmur
I like whores from other countries if you're anything to go by
Smelling his abomination and stink on her
The averted eyes of those who should care
The doctor asking; do you usually like rough sex?
Teachers asking; why do you need an extension on your homework?
Not being able to drive downtown 14 years later and they say
It's okay in time you get over everything
She stands with her eyes shut and can see it all
The prosecutor says; Miss you have amazing recall
We decided to press ahead with your testimony because your story
matches word for word ten years later
They may ask you if you wanted to be with a homeless man because
you were an unfulfilled lesbian but try not to get upset
He looks at her across the room he is at least five years younger and
incongruously handsome
She wants to be sick
He tells the court she was lying on the floor passed out, Sir I don't
know who drugged her I was just trying to help
How did your semen end up inside her vagina? Your claw marks on
her skin?
She woke up and wanted me to do her, you see, she's beautiful, I'm
a man, how could I say no?
(There is something else he did that neither of them tells)
Secrets within secrets
People posing as hollow shells
He is African American and her suburban friends ask
If she's scared of black men now

She replies; I'm not scared of anything anymore but that's a lie
All men scare her
And color is irrelevant
At the same time, she sees the system
Prosecute those who cannot afford and release those who can
Sickeningly she feels guilty for causing his incarceration
Even as he earned it himself
The reason for this, she tells no one
She feels she is not worth it
(Nobody should go to prison for raping me even with HIV)
The self-hate is a hidden poison below the surface
When people compliment her on being strong
She wants to scream; Rape isn't just rape
It lasts
It endures long past the crime
Till the crime becomes
How we feel about ourselves
In the quiet hours of the day when we sit unguarded

If "Boys Will Be Boys," Then Girls Are Allowed to be Angry

Raney Simmon

The saying,
"Boys will be boys,"
Strikes an angry chord within my soul.

It speaks as a reminder,
To the pain and suffering,
Women have endured by men.

It reminds me,
Of the times,
I was
Bullied,
Groped,
Assaulted by men.

Who thought nothing
About the harm they had caused.

Who see women
As nothing but sexual objects
To thrust their desires upon.

Then live on,
As if they've done nothing wrong.

Continuing to go unpunished,
Because nobody believes us
When we speak.

But I refuse,
To stay silent.

Because I am tired
Of women's voices,
Being unheard.

So I refuse,
To be another
Silenced victim.

Instead,
I choose
To be angry.

Because our voices,
Remain unheard.

Because justice,
Remains to be found.

So if,
"Boys will be boys,"
Then us girls—
Us women,
Are allowed
To be angry.

Lioness Roar
Dena M Daigle

Nothing could ever prepare me for the things I've had to endure, but I will no longer be silenced by fear. You will hear my lioness roar!

Dena M. Daigle | Lioness Roar

Broken Bones
kkc

In the back with the decrepit bones
sits you just staring blankly ahead

Cold gaze of yours
couldn't focus on me this day
never saw my small self then either
Does not seeing make it better?

I always had these eyes fixed though

Watching
For
You
To
Come

Not one time
did your cracked lips
push out my name

Dry throat of yours accented the grunts loudly
Trespassing sounds pierced my eardrums and
they still bleed from the memories

My skin feels the harsh touch,
it never left, it always lingers there

From

Rough, cracked hands that pushed me
so that I had to taste gritty dirt

Also

Do you know what filthy dust smells like?
Nostrils of mine are still filled with the grime

I never told your precious secret

But

It appears that time found out

You are breaking by the day
You are crumbling by the night

Is it fun sitting with filthy skeletons
in your own closet?

Do not think I will tell where you are
Stay there and wait

Sticks and stones will surely

Break. Your. Bones.
It will be your turn to eat the dirt

Buried Alive
Tanya Shukla

The secluded grave where I was buried
alive, has now a majestic oak- tree
standing tall and strong, spreading
it's lean long branches, encompassing
engulfing, everything falling in its way.
Its roots penetrating the very core of
mother Earth, keeping me warm inside
her womb, it will bear fruits for thousands
of years, after you and me will be gone
silk cloth that was shoved into my mouth,
To silence my voice has now millions of
listeners, on its humble branches migratory
birds from south chirp and listen to the
softer heartbeats from beneath the ground,
in its formidable bark dwells a civilization
Of insects of various kinds, nests of birds
where new lives are germinating from
yellowish shells, eager to spread my voice
in all directions, maggots have done a
perfect job by nibbling away the sinful flesh
Peeling it from the frightening skeleton,
horrifying the scavengers and the species
of one particular mankind, through me
tall elephant grass is making its way like
a bushfire enflaming, an entire row of houses
In the town where dwell women of my kind,
silenced, chained and buried in the very walls
decorated with nude portraits of Victorian
virgins, for mine and their voices, will echo
forever in the hollow misty damp air

Sister nature will take its own course
merging together with us, for we will

resurrect and rise from our nameless
graves in times to come, for we are not
dead but patiently waiting for our turn.

"I think this Anthology is important because
it is the voice of men and women who have
chosen to be the victors instead of the
victims. It is a collection of courage and
strength. It will provide support to those
who have also found their voice and to the
ones who are still searching. It will show
them that they are not alone. We see you.
We support you. We are here. You are not
alone."

Emily James

The Silent
Ann Stolinsky

"Me too." Women and men have finally been able to openly grieve about their tainted childhoods, have finally been able to share their stories of pain and humiliation. Have finally been given a voice that's being heard around the world.

I can't share my story.

I'm the face of the children who aren't on Facebook. I'm the poster child for the life these men and women left behind. I am the voiceless innocent.

I am the embodiment of the lied to, the hurt, the scared. I am told I cannot tell my story for fear of retribution, against me, against my parents, against anyone I love. I am the face of the children who hide from their own parents at night. Me, I am not a whole child.
I am the teenager who is excited to be going on my first date, only to be date raped. I will spend the rest of my days in a psychiatrist's office, alone. I will never trust.

I am the kindergartener who's been told by my father never to divulge "our secret." I go to school puzzled and ashamed, wondering if anyone in my class has a father who loves them like mine loves me.

I am the child whose growth has been stunted by the horrors I cannot describe because I haven't learned the words for them yet.
I am the child who is still experiencing, in my present, in my current state, the life that others are opening up about, their pasts.

"Me too." Someone please spread the word for the silent innocents. "Me too.

Me Too
Elizabeth Beaver

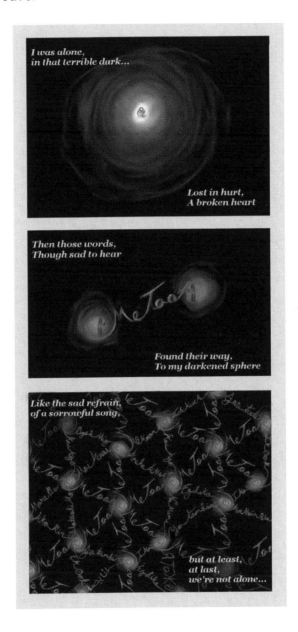

it's time
Matthew D Eayre

why are you so afraid to tell the
whole story?
you've paid for the words.

say them.

Matthew D Eayre | it's time

Expiation
Dena M. Daigle

My innocence was stripped from my supple flesh by blood-stained hands,
desecrated upon white cotton sheets.
I staggered upon trembling limbs from the depths of hell that day and straight into the void where nothing and no one could ever hurt me again.
A part of me was lost, battered and broken,
and I wasn't sure if I would ever see that little girl again.
My demons became my only companions and they begged me to open up my mouth;
but I screamed in silence instead.
I sought relief from a hypodermic needle and love in the form of thinly disguised misogyny.
But my spirit, she is fierce; she is a warrior of light and she will no longer be silenced.
I have risen from those ashes; a phoenix ascended from my ruins with a message to carry upon charred wings:
you may have defiled my temple, but you will never steal my crown.

Birth of Bones
Stephanie Bennett-Henry

I was lips split, pinned down, throat wearing a necklace, custom made with your handprint. I was fear searching blindly for my own breath that never promised me anything other than a swear from your eyes of all the ways it could be stolen. I was a paper doll, tiny stature, threatening to break like porcelain proving its pieces. I was, "yes, sir" carrying the weight of the world on top of me, bearing secrets like promises not to ever break. I was the straight faced, everything is fine smile, with hands in my pants that never learned the meaning of stop and no, only yes and go and go and.. are you done yet? Please be done. Please let it be the last time. Please god, please anyone… hear me. I was silence never heard, a voice that never spoke... until now. AND I REFUSE TO EVER WHISPER AGAIN. Your skeletons woke to the sound of my fists unclenched, my scream is a siren that cannot be silenced anymore, I am bringing bones to your door.

An open letter to the pillagers of my purity
Dena M. Daigle

I wish I could tell you how badly you destroyed me, but I don't even know your name. Yet because of you that I have flinched every time a man has ever touched my delicate skin. Because of you, I have built walls around my heart so high that most give up on the ascent before ever coming close to reaching the summit. Because of you, I wouldn't know real love if it arrived in a pretty box with a bow on top and a gift-tag that said "this is the good stuff." Every single time I was betrayed by someone who claimed to love me, my spirit crumbled a little bit more. Yet because of you, I was so afraid of being alone that I settled for far less than I ever deserved.

Because of you, my self-worth was measured on a scale always tilted in the favor of another. And because of you, I have allowed my flesh to be desecrated at the hands of merciless cowards who had no intention of kneeling at my temple. Because of you, I constantly apologize for things I have no control over; sometimes even for my own existence. Because of you...well, who am I kidding? It is ALL because of you.

You see, it is because of you that I fight with every fiber of my being to heal. It is because of you that I share the power of my voice for all the broken spirits who cannot find the strength and courage to speak. And it is because of you, and every wrong path you led me to, that I found my purpose!

Although you annihilated my innocence and changed my life forever, I wish you no harm. I actually hope you are doing quite well. I hope that you have a very long life ahead of you with an excellent memory; and I hope your demons keep you company every night as you lay your head on your pillow. I pray that somehow, some way, you read this someday and see the face of the brave little girl you almost destroyed. You couldn't silence me forever.

253

After ... you know ...
Petru J. Vilijoen

Considering grace:
reserve, perhaps a
patience;
certainly mercy
relief then: shifting an
ache
lodged hard, deep as
memory

**Petru J. Vilijoen | After
... you know ...**

Henini
Katharine Love

i'm mourning the loss of my tribe.
i'm mourning the loss of my dream
of sharing a holiday meal
with all my relations.
i'm mourning the loss of
adopting a child from china,
giving me that second
chance at becoming a good mother.
i'm mourning the loss of my innocence.
i'm mourning the loss of all
my illusions.
i'm mourning the loss of
my last hiding place.
i have lost the battle,
that has raged on
for so long,
i can't even remember who
started the war.
i surrender.
i live now in this
arid desert,
nothing here but
stardust and sand.
"i am alive,
i am alive!"
said my still throbbing heart
to the sand, to the
sky, and to me.
here i am.
Henini

Find me
Laurie D. Wise

There is no quiet in the wicked night
Where shadows are birthed
Writhing through sleep shrouded eyes
Rousing her into aphotic collection
Impelled toward dark thorn forest
Seizing her decrepit parody
Limbs whip her pallid face
A splatter of red
Highlights her gaunt essence
Believing hue can conceive dream
Silently licking blood not blood
From her lips~
Don't go
Don't go
Don't go

Her world is on fire
She walks with the dead
Beguiling her way
An orphan in scorched gown
Calloused feet her only confidant
Ashes expose the course
Fate gave without cause
Washed to dirt in places where ghosts
Followed too close
Effigies suck her last gasp of air
And whisper through wisps
Of singed hair~
You are lost
You are lost
You are lost

She is sick from pining
Existing of the old, fragile and frail
Archaic from ages of bondage
Possessed by fiends of the inferno
Though her bones rattle, crack and crumble
Resiliency is her birthright
Fetal face shut tight in womb
Sightlessness a requisite for survival
Evolution ameliorates and amends
Progress has befallen unseen
Open her eyes~
Keep looking
Keep looking
Keep looking

Promises of hope linger in her ears
A source of the auspicious
She cleaves the treasure foretold
A prophecy brighter than fire
A gift to remediate spiritual anguish
The dull ache of her soul
She longs with nothing to long for
Show her the path
To divine manifestation
Within her~
Find me
Find me
Find me

Never a Chance
Madame K Poetess

You want to know who I was before I
became the person that I am. The person
before I became distant, damaged, closed off
& broken. Do you want to hear how I was happy all the time
& tears never fell from my eyes except for the times
when I watched a movie where the dog dies
or when I had to let go of someone
I loved by saying a final goodbye.
Do you want to hear that my life was all
rainbows & butterflies once upon a time
& that over the years I took a wrong turn
somewhere, only to end up right where I am?
Truth is, I don't know who I was supposed to be or
who I could have been, all I know is that one side of my life,
as far back as I can remember,
allowed me to be a happy child, where I could smile,
play & forget, & then I had to return to the other side
of my life, my reality & I had to suffer in silence,
witnessing years of violence amongst my family
& within my own home; it was brutal.
Having body parts of multiple men
reach places that stripped me of my innocence,
over & over again; A nightmare that you can never forget
no matter what you do to make them stop
They're always there.
Far too young to save myself
& yet, no one came to my rescue
when I cried out for help. So I stopped
crying out. Eventually I learnt I had to save myself.
So here I am, the person that I am
& the person that I was, doesn't exist because
she was never given a chance to live

what should have been a different life.
So I am who I am, & if the only good thing
I can walk away from it all with
is that I have been able to help
someone else find strength in themselves
to not give up - then all of what I have been through
At least went towards a good cause.

Wayward Daughter
V.J. Knutson

Back and forth, I travel
searching for her -
retrace every bend,
curve, detour –

Back to the water,
the sand, the beach
where I lost her –

Haunted by
those velvet brown eyes -
bedroom eyes, they said,
men with greedy loins,
calculating –

I lost her
to the lure
of alcohol,
to the beating
of drums,
in smoky corners
so far removed
from the purity
of her dreams…

It's been an arduous
journey, some days
so lost in the daze
of forgetting;
I cycle back,
memories of manhood
exposed, egos craving

stroking, how I learned
what men wanted,
learned to numb
the disappointment
with fast-talk
and all-nighters,
suppressed tears,
discovered that words
hold no promise,
and water is deep

And going within
is a dark, foreboding place,
and worth is shrouded by the shame
of discovering that even the father
I adored was not as he appeared,
and that this primal urge for mating
was a trap designed to eradicate
my beauty not enhance it....

I need to find her -
hold her afloat
in sacred waters -
help her feel the healing
light of a thousand women's hearts
all bleeding as one, all warped by
the same convoluted messages
of womanhood -

that lust is sinful
and copulation a man's domain,
and that in order to be wed, she must
forego her own nature, tame
the wild, settle
for loss of control...

But as much as I travel
these lonely roads, I cannot
find her; the traces of her innocence
washed away by the tides,
now lines on my aging face...

If you see her, please
hold her close, protect her
from beasts, hold her until
the beauty of her being
is solid knowledge, and shame
has been vanquished;
teach her that being a vessel
for man's release in not
her only purpose.

Finding Love in a #MeToo Watershed Moment
Michèle Duquet

There is something happening… An energetic shift is taking over our collective consciousness. This is it… we think. The moment everything changes… we hope. Each story, opening our hearts a little bit more. Each shared memory, a reminder of how sensitive, breakable and beautiful the human heart truly is.

The dam finally broke under pressure, and the painful truth of days gone by is now bursting through our carefully constructed version of reality.

What we couldn't feel then, we are feeling now.

Navigating anxious sleepless nights however, waking up at 2:00 am filled with triggered emotions surfacing from long forgotten memories… this is not the #MeToo watershed moment I had in mind.

It's 2:00am. I wake up in a panic, blood rushing through my veins, my heart pounding in my chest and throat. A memory resurfaces. I'm a 22-year-old model on a location shoot for a big magazine and I'm being groped by the photographer. Out of nowhere he sneaked up on me from behind and shoved both of his hands in my front pockets, reaching down to grope me, uninvited. Unwanted.

But tonight, I'm not shocked or frozen. I am furious. This isn't the first time I remember this… so why am I so angry tonight, and scared…? I feel panic rising, I feel myself resisting looking at a snapshot emerging from the shadows of my past…

Suddenly I'm 16 and this same photographer rips open my blouse in front of everyone as I stand posing for a jeans ad campaign alongside a lineup of young women also forced to reveal too much cleavage. Click-click-click goes the camera, freeze-framing us in our

263

low-cut blouses and tight jeans for the sheer sexiness of it, the shock of it: the selling of it. I say nothing. I smile for the camera. We all do. I was paid a lot of money to stand there, unbuttoned, in a big jeans billboard campaign. But I was 16. Only 16. I had been violated and thought nothing of it, thought it would seem too prudish of me to say something. I was very successful, had been on many magazine covers. I could've said something, but I didn't. I went into survivor mode. I went into shock. I froze. At other times I'd stood up for myself, was assertive, strong, vocal, but not then. Not at 16. And until this mid-night #MeToo moment, I'd completely forgotten that it was the same photographer who had assaulted me 6 years later.

Yet here it is decades later, click-click-click the photographs of my past streaming by, landing in my pounding heart for the very first time… as I feel now what I couldn't feel then. I was violated at 16, and then again at 22 by the same man, both moments now flashing back before me in the dead of night.

Many more photographs stream by, a picture-show telling the same story, over and over again. But none affect me in quite the same way. After the age of 22, I began speaking up. I became tough and very vocal. I often wondered why that was… now I know. My 16 and 22-year-old selves had somehow formed an alliance in the dark corners of my subconscious that let me know, "it's not you. It's him."

That is when, unexpectedly, tenderly, love shined its light on the past. I love that 16-year-old. That 22-year-old. That 35-year-old. That 41-year-old. They all live in me and I love them all. I love them for braving to come out of the dark, for breaking through my resistance, my suppression, to let me know that "It's not you. It's not yours."

As I embrace what travels through me during this mid night slideshow, I awaken to the profound recognition of just how beautiful and sensitive the human heart is. We've all been hurt. We all carry within us our own version of that 16-year-old who went into hiding, not to resurface again for decades. I can love my anger, my pain, my fear and my silence because I know I am not alone. I have my sisters and my brothers standing with me, side-by-side, feeling and healing what has been reawakened through this collective shift in our heart-consciousness.

Those of us reliving our #MeToo memories are waking up to a new reality, where we can see ourselves and our human condition with new depth, clarity and love; where accepting and loving our anger, fear, panic and silence becomes possible because *this* is our *healing moment.*

It's 3:00 am... I can hear my spirit's wisdom as I listen to my heart. "Your feelings are beautiful" it tells me. "It's safe to feel now" it whispers.

And I know. In my heart, I know. This is our moment, the moment we stand together for love... and together, we heal.

Little Girl
April Yvette

to the little girl still inside of me
i know many failed to protect you
the ones you trusted with no hesitation
only to have your innocence ripped away
left with blood-stained panties and sheets
leaving you terrified and all alone to cry
for help silently through pleading eyes
secretly wanting to be able to grow wings
and fly far away – i was not there yet to
wrap my arms around you and slay the
monsters who preyed upon you – i am sorry
i was not able to be the woman i am today
to be there for you yesterday – i tried to
bury it all, the atrocities and at times you
just to be able to believe i was not to blame
to heal wounds i still did not understand
i am sorry i shut you away but i did not
know any other way – i hope you can forgive
me and know now i have a voice not for the
woman i am now but for the child i was – i
promise you i will never let us live in silence
again – i am here for you and one day my
sweet little girl who still resides deep in me
i hope you will be able to be healed and
smile knowing you can live without fear – to
walk in the light – letting me give you
back all which was stolen

Intertwined
Irma Do

The woman I am
Is the woman I was
The quiet one
The smart one
The bookworm
The one who ran a high school mile in 20 minutes.

The woman I am
Is the woman I was
The hands in my back pocket,
I can conquer the world,
Let the party begin,
I can pull off an A paper in 4 hours Co-ed
Who wasn't self aware enough
Who wasn't practiced enough
To know alcoholic lies.

The woman I am
Is the woman I was
The trusting in a good world
How did this happen to me
Despite my negative words
Against my feminist will
It must be my fault
Forgive me, understand me lover.

The woman I am
Is the woman I was
The grieving mother
The don't get too close so it doesn't hurt mother
The oh it could be fun and easy mother
The I didn't realize boys were so different mother

The woman I am
Is the woman I was Angry and hurt
Confused yet hopeful
Spurned into action
Despite fears of rejection.

I am the intersection of
My gender
My ethnicity
My religion
My race
The intertwining of identity and history
The woman I am
Is the woman I was
Is the woman I will become

Put the newspaper down first, this is bound to make a mess
Georgia Park

The next time I have sex

(I'll invite someone from my contacts list
Doesn't much matter which)

I will light candles

And spread newspaper

On my floor

murmuring threats like

"I'm going to devour you whole,"

I will have paints

We can dip our hands into

Then touch each other all over
As evidence that I've let this happen,

Our touches will leave

The prettiest of colors
I will do this

Just as soon as I can

Surrender myself again
Someday, its really going to be

"This Anthology speaks for so many who cannot. It screams out the pain of voices that have been silenced by fear, by power, by blame. Being a part of this allows me to say, "I see you. And I stand with you. And your battle is important." People who go through this type of trauma will forever have scars and wounds that won't mend. But, by coming together and voicing our outrage and our own experiences, we join as one group of collective voices who refuse to go unheard. I am honored to be included and to be able to hold hands with the brave warriors who will not back down."

Ashley Jane

Intensity
Petru J. Viljoen

On Lessons (or, How to Scream Without Waking the Neighbors)

R.S. Williams

i learned to smile in dead languages the night i realized the words leaving my mouth seemed to have no pulse (i'd always heard that people with life still beating in their stomachs will always listen very closely to something when they think the heart in it has stopped).

later, i found tough, whole flowers bursting beneath my skin from seeds of tales heavy with instructions for my behavior, and they were forced like horror into me as a child; the thorns that pushed up from such broken stories found it a simple matter to pinch through fractures pounded into me during the time i shattered beneath hands that moved faster than the fear in "no". these days, those thorns have since began protecting me, too, for they love me the same as they would something beautiful and holy that never knew enough to try blooming for them.

now, i am teaching myself to heal, especially on the sunnier days when my own laughter is rounder than i am. i will give myself permission to cure the big world inside of me, even as it still splits apart with the understanding that tears stand a better chance of being seen when they're put to use as diamonds in a crown flashing with false joy rather than when they're leaving behind trails that lead south on a dirty face intent on breaking.

and at last, i'm beginning to remember the strength passing through my veins like a gift from an age that's never forgotten my people; it's been tempering me into armor, even before the first of the fists in my chest burst from my throat with my voice clutched high and tight like gold stolen from a tomb.

i am only now learning to rise, but i am more eager than ever to admit that i carry within me something like good, proud power in places that should never be filled with anything else—and it's the kind of might that will never stop whispering war against those doubts that would wear my face while waving me like a white flag in a world thick with canons firing things like "hush" and "if you tell them…".

"This anthology is meaningful to me because it's an issue that has been silenced for too long. It is time to raise the volume, put our voices together and scream it loud and clear. Sometimes you have to make everyone uncomfortable enough to finally stop and LISTEN."

Stephanie Bennett-Henry

You were always brave
N. R. Hart

You were brave as you fashioned your own crown
out of tarnished jewels found amongst scattered toys
and worn out rag dolls held tight by a little girl
too scared to let go.
You were brave as you hid your pain underneath layers
and layers of pink tulle and lace, scars left behind
by big hands that tried to break you, making you feel
small and silencing you with too many secrets.
You were brave holding back your tears welling up in
your eyes, too afraid to blink or they would fall, blink
again and they would come pouring out. These little
pearl droplets held sacred by a sadness so deep you
safeguarded with your soul.
And, you were brave even though they tried to make
you feel weak and they almost succeeded, until one day
you realized you had the power to love yourself first,
become your own hero, seal your own fate.
So you kissed your own darkness hello and said goodbye
to the years of guilt you carried and began wearing your
crown like the queen you are. And, you were always
brave.

Spaces Between Trees
Mary A. Rogers Glowczwskie

Details evade my memory
Ashes scattered on the wind
A game of Hide-and-Seek
Years of my life, once lived, now gone

What remained stayed
Like an unwanted guest
Taking residence within my soul
Speaking the same words again and again

Unlovable
Unwanted
Unworthy
Unloved

I remember once praying to die
Or maybe it was once times one million
Burrowing deep within myself
Tangled feelings and web of lies

The Confusion
The Fear
The Debilitating Sadness
The Rage Running Red Deep Within My Veins

And, yet, in that space, I found the light
The greatest gift given to me by you

My Abuser
My Molester
My Oppressor
My Rapist

For I learned to swim the ocean
As waves broke across my soul
I learned of a depth – vast and deep
Where only the brave dared to go

Immersed in that darkness, I found a light
Where hope grew like wildflowers
Spaces between the trees
I found magic in words whilst thoughts floated on wings

And I finally understood

Why the Caged Bird Sings

Refuse to be afraid

Claire, from CK words and thoughts

And much like
Little Red Riding Hood
I refuse to be afraid
of the woods
or the scary unknown
that resides in the dark
Instead I feel
safe and free there
seeing as most bad things
actually happen indoors
by people you know
and sometimes even
with the lights turned on

**Claire, from CK words and thoughts |
Refuse to be afraid**

bad bitch, make him nervous.
Samantha Lucero

I'm happily divorced, I have twin girls, and I'm the type of person that needs to create, who was born to create, who feels that whisper on their neck in the night to make something, leave something behind, break it, build it, burn it... but I never wanted to create a life, especially not two of them. That's the tragic irony of my predicament; shit happens. And now here I am writing this with an existential guilt that I'll carry for the rest of my days in the circus we're in. Here I am writing this with a fear that prevents me from having the ability to turn my back on my daughters when any man's around, even men I know. A fear that made me teach them the word *vagina*, a fear they'll be too pretty, a fear they'll be alone one night with me not there to tell them *not to listen to that bullshit, he's just trying to get you alone*, a fear that's beginning to steel me against the day they tell me something I never wanted to hear. A fear that they'll be afraid like I am, on guard, never letting anything into my shriveled husk of a heart. So when they say to me "mama, the dark is scary" I say back to them, "Don't worry, I'm the scariest thing in this dark," and for now, they believe me, because for now... it's true.

The tenacity of my urge to create and that longing tucked within me, nurtured in that very aforementioned dark, made the roots of the cosmos shudder and listen in their own satirical way. I have double the trouble; double the girls. We're trouble, right?

Don't we attract it? Don't we ask for it with dolly-pink lips smudged by a Pabst Blue Ribbons' gutter, or a comely sheepish grin under office halogens, or in a delicate fabric skirt hiked just a sip above the knee? The ones in fishnets are really asking for it, but the ones in the military uniforms are asking for it, too, which, mind you, experience retaliation almost always for reporting sexual crimes. But those simpering nuns alone in the Dark Ages huddled into a concrete corner past a nave and near a pulpit praying for the privateers to leave what they think is the only sacred thing about them in fact, well, aren't they asking for it, too? Girls are trouble, right? Haven't they always been?

We've been hanged, burned, shackled, torn open, sold, raped, abused, beat, tortured, laughed at, humiliated, overlooked, ignored; and you better not complain about it, better not 'run your mouth' or you're a bitch. All because we're trouble; all because we talk too much, and when we talk, we don't know what we're talking about because we're women, or maybe we read too much, but we don't read the right things, or we stick up for ourselves, but we do it in a way that isn't gentle enough for the soft hearts of the hard heads of men, or maybe we have something that somebody else wants; that somebody else thinks that they can take. And sometimes, they do. And then we're never who we thought we were, and we're never who we were, before, again. We're something in between.

Trauma is a lot like death; it brings you out of yourself and out of your own body. You somehow become a prisoner within your own skin, when all this time you thought your bones were the best hideout, and yet someone found the fucking bat cave. It brings you closer to death to survive a trauma, because you begin to leave the world for a little while. The world wasn't what you thought it was, shit, sometimes it's exactly what you knew the fuck it was and that doesn't matter, because trauma is always different. There's always another thread of you to snip, another button to pop, another seam to rip. Some extract themselves slower than others from the world after trauma, but everybody leaves and sinks within him or herself for a while; some never leave the pool. Isolation is warm water; it's a fucking jetted tub. And in that incubation you can get lost forever. The warmth of its safety makes sense as much as the sting of its loneliness hurts.

I usually use riddles in my poetry so that, like a spell, it summons the right things when the right feelings are involved in repeating the words within one's mind. They say the words don't matter, that the intention does; my intention is to make you angry. I hope I'm doing that.

The world won't be kind to my daughters. Neither will it be kind to your daughters. We are all, as women, daughters. We won't all be mothers, we won't all be sisters, but we are and always will be daughters, and the world will never be kind.

Neither was the world kind to me. I am a living scar. I am a jagged edge, a hole, a bunch of pieces stapled together, but fuck, I'm still alive. I'm too alive sometimes. No matter how much I've wanted to die, wished for it to happen, tried to make it happen, I'm still here. It's been because of what other people have done to me or forced on me, the stains they put in places I can't reach to clean, the graves they dug between my legs and in the back of my mind. Too fat, too thin, too pretty, too ugly, you wanted it, are you sure that happened, are you sure you weren't flirting, are you sure he did that, are you sure, are you sure. Am I sure? Fuck you. You wanted me dead and I'm here. You're here too if you're reading this and bitch, that's the best revenge. They wanted you gone. To them you were nothing: be something to yourself and live. You're still in the game. You're still in the show and it's been going on and on and on. You're a bad bitch. Make him nervous.

My ex-husband, the father of the twin girls I mentioned up there, and an ex-husband for good reasons, finds it highly offensive when my more assertive and stubborn daughter, who's nearly three, sticks up for herself. She doesn't want to be nuzzled by him. She doesn't want a kiss. She doesn't want a hug. She wants him to go away. Sometimes, she'll say 'dad, I don't like you right now!' and he blames me, says she's too much like me, says she talks like that because I do. It's harmless, he wants a hug, but if she doesn't start practicing how to shove off unwanted attention, she never will. I tell him to think of it that way. Think of it as steeling her now so she'll grow up as hard as she can, but tender enough still to love.

When she comes home from visiting him someday, or perhaps from school, saying she got into trouble for *running her mouth*, I'll tell her to run it even louder next time and to never listen anybody that tells her to shut up. When she uses bad words in school I'll laugh because I'm the one who taught them to her, especially if it's in defense of who she is. I was always so afraid to be me when I was young, so the first thing I'm teaching my daughters is to be themselves.

And that they can be the scariest thing in the dark, too.

The Nothing You Made
Sarah Doughty

"No matter how hard you tried,
you could never break my spirit."

It took years, but I clawed through the ruins that was my existence. I picked up the salvageable pieces and slowly built myself back up from nothing. The nothing you made of me. I found new pieces to build my foundations, and tossed away the ones you stacked on unstable ground.

And this. This is me now. This is me, living. This is me, standing on my own. No matter how hard you tried, you could never break my spirit.

Still the sun

Claire, from CK words and thoughts

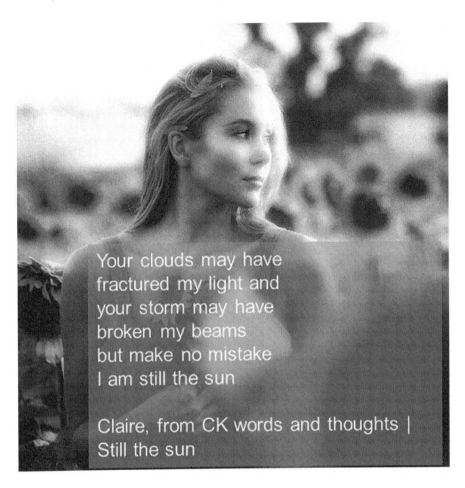

Your clouds may have
fractured my light and
your storm may have
broken my beams
but make no mistake
I am still the sun

Claire, from CK words and thoughts |
Still the sun

I Stayed Silent
April Yvette

From an early age, my innocence was ripped away. The first was from my father. A man who was to protect me, to guide me, to love me. But in reality he was a monster and I feared every moment with him. There were countless others who had their way with me all before I was even ten years old. I blamed myself because I was always told if I was a good girl then these atrocities would have never happened. I stayed silent.

Do you know what it is like to grow up knowing you are to remain silent? This is when I put on my mask for the first time to convince everyone I was fine. There were red flags everywhere, but no one ever did a damn thing to save me. If no one would save me, then I knew no one would believe me. I stayed silent.

I was told to sit up straight, act like a lady, smile, don't cry or else. One memory stands out of the way my father posed me in a set of pictures, my mother was impressed with the photography. But she did not know the horror I endured before and after those pictures. In those pictures, in my eyes, you can see a plea for help. I stayed silent.

I continued to take the blame. Brainwashed, I believed it was me that caused the molestations, the rapes and the physical abuse. I was told I was nothing, I would be nothing, I was to be used and will just be a whore. At one point I did become very sexually promiscuous, I was becoming what I was told I would be. I didn't know anything else or any other way. This was the only way to be loved and accepted. I stayed silent.

I slept with men because I believed it was all they wanted. I pushed away anyone who would get close. I became a functioning drug addict, suffered from anorexia, bulimia, multiple failed suicide attempts. I hated to look at my reflection in the mirror. At the time I didn't know I was filled with a plethora of mental illnesses. I was proving to everyone I would be nothing, I would just be a tool to be used. I stayed silent.

I carried pain on my flesh, in my bones, in my eyes that everyone still ignored. Up until 1999, when I was 29 years old, I was still a victim to assaults, rapes and physical beatings from ones who knew I would not breathe a word. I was compliant, because it was all I knew. I was led to believe that a woman is to do what she is told. All I could hear each time in my head was my father's voice saying I was to blame, I caused this. I stayed silent.

But the same year, it all changed, I met my third husband. I spilled it all out to him, he understood, he wanted to help. He helped me get into therapy. I learned about myself. I learned I wasn't to blame, I was worthy, I had a voice. From that point on, I took back my power. A power I never had, a power which was ripped away too young. All it took was one person to see a lifetime of pain, not turn a blind eye and saw me as a person. I began to heal, I began to grow, I began to breathe a life I was denied. I was no longer silent.

I now had my voice, I don't belong to anyone, I was a person. I found my worth, my life, my body was mine and mine alone. I took back my innocence with strength. I learned to love myself. But most of all I forgave myself for believing all those years I was to blame. It took me 29 years to do this. But I promised myself I will never be a victim, nor a survivor, but a warrior. I will never remain silent again.

Backbone
Sabrina Escorcio

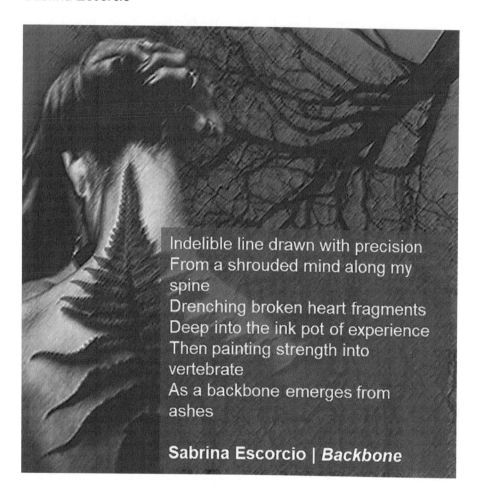

Indelible line drawn with precision
From a shrouded mind along my
spine
Drenching broken heart fragments
Deep into the ink pot of experience
Then painting strength into
vertebrate
As a backbone emerges from
ashes

Sabrina Escorcio | *Backbone*

Bleeding Rose
Michelle Schaper

Sometimes I now caress
my own velvet thighs
I spent way too many years
listening to a mirror's lies
I could still see, the bruises you left me
they stained my soul
for so long I tasted my own blood dripping through each beat of my
heart
leaving a gaping hole
But now the blossoming
has finally broken free
closing gaps behind
new growth found inside of me
And every time I sip on pain
through straws of memories
I no longer swallow pride or taste the blame
I've learned to bloom
each time I bleed.

Unleashed
A. Shea (Angie Waters)

My heart will not die
for the thieves
who took innocence
and pure beliefs
for their own vices.
Used and abused,
I survived this
and I will not be reduced
in the least.
I am fire
and I will be unleashed.

A. Shea | Unleashed

Dearly Beloved
Amanda J. Forrester

Let us now kill
each other with blades
we bled to wield.
We shall kill
the women we love
     yes, love
and kill them with our words, laws
I will call my father and he will
be pleased.
My mother will be pleased if
he is please.
She will accept our blades – obedient
to her vows
to his rule

and we shall be free

to ban together for our own
sake, the sake
of our children, though
half will be murdered as they sleep, wake
to see their funerals online.

in time

they will inherit our blades
that murdered them, turning
toward each other with blood
in their eyes

yes, let us now proceed
and lift our inked blades

and cast our ballots.

"We have been silent too long. We were afraid of blame, of reprisal, of being labeled liars. But a window has opened for us, and it's urgent that we speak now. Sexual abuse has left many of us with P.T.S.D. and thousands of dollars spent on therapy. There is power and healing in speaking out. This Anthology is important to all of us, women and men alike."

Lola White

Empowered
Emily James

I didn't just take back my power
I cut it from your grip
With glass from the house
You were living in

Emily James | Empowered

Phoenix
Megha Sood

When you rip me apart
shred my feathers into bits and pieces
scrape till it reaches the bone
and laugh at my misery
smug over my plight
when you take your bloody knuckles
dipped in my blood
and smear all over my face
trying to write your song of victory
Never forget for a moment
my silence doesn't mean
submission
my anger doesn't mean
arrogance
my freedom doesn't mean
privilege
my blood smeared face doesn't mean
shame
I'm **Phoenix**
born out of a
fire
rage
pain
are my bone marrow
I rise from the ashes of the
naysayers and blood mongers
I'm crucified,
to give wisdom to the ignorant
I can give birth to a soul
infuse flesh and blood
to make you mortal
You can carve out

your pound of flesh out of me
but you can not touch the light
which makes me glow from within.

"Participating in the 'We Will Not be Silenced
Anthology' allowed me to bestow upon my inner child
the greatest gift of all - the voice she never
had. Speaking my truth out loud to the world has
been a very humbling and human experience which,
at times, has left me feeling very vulnerable,
subjected to judgment and ridicule; but I now rise to
the occasion with fortitude and gratitude alike,
knowing that I stand among so many brave and
beautiful souls willing to speak their most sacred
truths and that gives me a sense of freedom, courage
and empowerment. I proudly stand beside my warrior
brothers and sisters as an unstoppable force of truth.
We will not be silenced!"

Dena M. Daigle

Rage
A. Shea (Angie Waters)

No one could hear
the violence
on my heart.
Screams that never
broke the silence
burned as quiet
as the stars
that saved me...
until they were rage.

A. Shea | Rage

Rise of the divine

Jesica Nodarse

We hid
In plain sight
In caves
Locking away the ancient knowledge and power passed down from
the stars themselves
Sometimes allowing the catching so we could spare others, to allow
the fruit of our womb to be safe
if for a spell
We tamed our beasts
Mostly in the presence of ignorance
Though men will tell you they domesticated us, and the clergy will
say they provided the tools
it was fathers who had no qualms in enforcing their rules
And so we became docile
Forgetful
Like furniture for a mans world
Property to be traded
Pawns in games of greed and shame
But the flame never went out
The embers dwelling in souls of the few and bold
And when we could finally whisper without going hoarse, we began
to speak
To write in secret
To make every effort to remember
To find the will to scream
These days we shout from mountaintops
We teach our daughters to roar and our boys to stomp along
We pick men who know our backs are as strong as theirs
And we honor them as they honor what lives within our breast
We make lifelong bonds with women who call themselves our tribe,
our kin
We will never forget again

We will only grow stronger
Our memory growing longer
Our voice will never again be silenced
We are more than ever before and the sky could never contain all we are yet to become
Watch as we take everything that has always belonged to us

The Unknown
C. O'Mahony

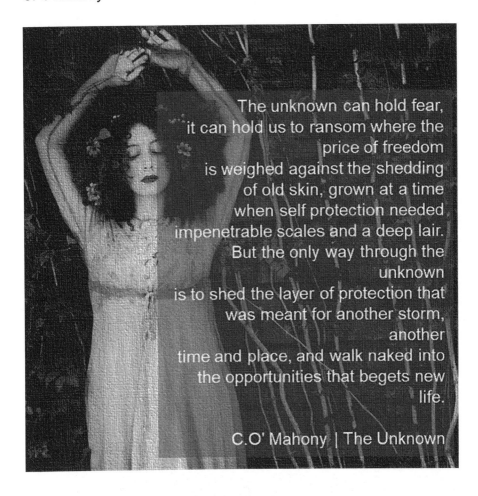

The unknown can hold fear,
it can hold us to ransom where the
price of freedom
is weighed against the shedding
of old skin, grown at a time
when self protection needed
impenetrable scales and a deep lair.
But the only way through the
unknown
is to shed the layer of protection that
was meant for another storm,
another
time and place, and walk naked into
the opportunities that begets new
life.

C.O' Mahony | The Unknown

Oceans cannot be poured into small bottles
Nikita Goel

Look at you, little woman
You are anything but ordinary.
People look at you and wonder what she is made of,
There are volcanoes erupting inside of you
Do not play small and dream little.
Oceans cannot be poured into small bottles,
You likewise cannot fit inside small hearts and minds.

Unleash the dragons breathing fire within you,
It is time to show the world who you are.
You are the most powerful Alchemist of the Universe
As you, transform unbearable pain into a thing of beauty
They tried to bury you and look what you became instead,
You rose from the ground and became a forest wildfire.

Untamed, Unconquered and Unstoppable,
You are the Lioness disguised as sheep and goats.
Take back your throne and reign like you mean it.
Let those wings break the ceiling and cut through the sky,
Do not worry about taking too much space, you own it all.

Author Biographies

Betty Albright has lived in the Pacific Northwest all her life and has been writing poetry since childhood. She is an environmental conservationist, an activist for the ERA, and the "Me Too" movement.

Grace Alexander survived growing up in a Quiverfull Dominionist cult and an abusive marriage. She now lives on a Uruguayan ranch with the love of her life, Amanda, with whom she runs a sanctuary for old and disabled dogs. Grace spends her days writing, cooking, and reading while surrounded by assorted children, dogs, cats, horses, goats, rabbits, and a fruit bat who lives in the barn.

Kindra M. Austin is an indie author and editor from Michigan. She's a founding member of Blood Into Ink, as well as Indie Blu(e). In addition to her advocacy for trauma survivors, Austin is an active supporter of the LGBTQ community, and has been published in the Mansfield Pride magazine.

"I am **R. Suresh Babu**. I have been working as a graduate teacher in English for the last 26 years in an organization called Navodaya Vidyalaya Samiti that predominantly caters to education and upliftment of rural children in India. I love poetry and I have contributed my poems to various groups on Facebook and other poetry websites. I hail from a place called Thiruvalla in Kerala, India. I am proud to be associated with this great anthology and cause."

Meg Baines: "I started writing at a young age to cope with anxiety, and it took having my daughter to save me from myself. I finally got brave, started *Snowhiite Writes*, and have continued writing in the hopes of helping people feel with what I believe are topics and emotions we have all experienced at one time or another."

Jane Basil is a writer who uses poetry to address and raise awareness of the burning issues of our times. She urges the downtrodden and abused to think of themselves as kintsugi; of their scars as purest gold, stronger than the flesh that was torn. Her scars have lost their sting, but she will not be silenced while others suffer.

Elizabeth Beaver is a writer and painter who lives in Charlotte, North Carolina with her handsome boyfriend and beautiful cat children. They have solid plans of living happily ever after. Elizabeth normally hides her poems in a box under her bed but thanks to the countless love and support of her friends and family is starting to open herself up to the world around her...Yuck, gross.

Stephanie Bennett Henry is a Texas-based mother, wife, writer, and poet. Her writing is packed with the type of pure emotion that can only be attained through life experience. Stephanie shares her words on most social media platforms, especially Facebook (PoetryofSL) and Instagram (stephaniebennetthenry). For more information please visit her website: https://stephaniebennetthenry.com/

Marilyn Rea Beyer has read poetry in public since the 1960s and began writing poems in 2005. She holds a Master's in Oral Interpretation of Literature from Northwestern University. Now retired, her varied career includes teaching, high tech, folk radio and working as PR Director for Perkins School for the Blind. A native Chicagoan she and her husband, author and filmmaker Rick Beyer, raised their two children in Lexington, Mass.

Suzette Bishop teaches at Texas A&M International University in Laredo. She's published three books and a chapbook and has a second chapbook, Jaguar's Book of The Dead, forthcoming. Her poems have appeared in many journals and anthologies, including The Antioch Review, 13th Moon, Concho River Review, The Little Magazine, and The Virago Book of Birth Poetry. One of her poems won the Spoon River Poetry Review Editors' Prize Contest.

Michelle Bradway is a fiction and creative non-fiction writer from a suburb near Philadelphia. As a Temple University undergraduate, she studied film as well as public relations, garnering an appreciation for these unique forms of storytelling—and the possibilities within them. Bradway writes professionally for non-profit organizations, but continues her personal writing in hopes of publishing pieces that encourage meaningful reflection and conversation about our shared and differing life experiences.

Cynthia Bryant claims poetry saved her life; that not only was poetry a safe way to transcend the terror and rage arising from childhood abuse, but also a tool to share and educate others. First published in 1997 by two important journals dealing with childhood sexual abuse, Cynthia Bryant has since been published in over 50 anthologies. Today Cynthia resides in Monterey where she hosts LAST SUNDAYS' Fishbowl Poetry. Read more at cynthialanebryant.com

Kathryn Buonantony is just your average Lady Lazarus attempting to squeeze the universe into a ball and be Spring. She is currently a candidate for a M.S. in Nonprofit Leadership at the University of Pennsylvania. Her plans for the future are to contribute to the empowerment of women and girls everywhere and to use words as a catalyst for change.

kkc holds her BS in Education and her MA in Curriculum and Instruction. After 30 years of working with children, she has returned to her first love of writing. She writes truths about people she knows and people she hasn't met yet. To date she has 20 published works and has written three books: Undefined, Sprinkles on Top, Smooth Rough Edges. The pen is the strongest tool we have. Peace.

tara caribou struggles with OCD-related depression, persistent repetition of thoughts, over-thinking, and apprehension. She is a Dreamer, has a vivid fantasy life within which she finds respite from reality, and is a voracious reader of hard science-fiction novels as well as poetry. Her love of nature is a major vehicle for her inspiration and peace. You can read her work at Raw Earth Ink.

Originally from Scotland, **Rebecca Cairns** is currently the editor for a wellness travel magazine in Hong Kong, where she has been based since 2015. A regular member of Peel Street Poetry Hong Kong, Rebecca has been writing poetry and fiction for over a decade. You can read more of her work on becca-ca.com or follow her adventures on Instagram @becca.ca.

My name is **Claire**, I am the founder of CK words and thoughts. I have been writing since I was a teen. In 2017, I started my Facebook page and shared my writing there. Since starting my page I have learned that my words let others know they are not alone in their situation. I'm honoured that 3 pieces have been chosen for this anthology so my voice can be heard.

Amanda.x.Coleman: "Word Lover. Stargazer. Over thinker. - Amanda grew up and lives on Cape Cod. She began writing at an early age, and began sharing her work on social media in 2015. She also has a passion for music, photography, and terrible puns. In her spare time she enjoys searching for synchronicities and looking for folds in the fabric of the universe."

Susan Conway published her debut novel, A Life of Whoredom in August of 2018. She has been featured in collaborative pieces with various authors and the Indie Blu(e) Collective. In her spare time, Susan enjoys blogging, gardening, cooking, and spending time with her family. For more about Susan M. Conway, you can find her at: www.facebook.com/TheGingerPost

Linda M. Crate's works have appeared in numerous anthologies and magazines both online and in print. She is the author of five books of poetry, a microchap, and the novel *Phoenix Tears* (Czykmate Books, June 2018).

Beth Couch grew up in the Deep South and has lived in Arkansas, Massachusetts, and Illinois, and currently resides in Washington, DC, where she writes for a financial firm. Previously, she taught writing and literature courses for 10 years, receiving her MA and PhD from Boston College. She began her writing career publishing academic essays on Victorian literature. She is a single mother who resides with her brilliant teenaged daughter.

Dawn D is a 40-something woman looking for her path through life, trying to extirpate herself from an emotionally, financially and sexually abusive marriage all the while discovering her wants, needs and deep rooted ME. Writing has helped heal many of her woes; Though the process is long, it's truly enlightening to realise she can help herself and support others at the same time.

Dena M. Daigle is an Indie wordsmith from New Orleans, Louisiana who began her love affair with words as a teenager. An advocate for survivors of sexual abuse, child abuse and drug addiction, she seeks to raise awareness and offer solace through her words. Her first book of poetry and prose, Scattered Ashes, was released in August, 2017 (Amazon.) Read Dena at Phoenix Ascended (WordPress) and on Facebook/Instagram as PhoenixAscended33.

French born poet **Candice Louisa Daquin** is the author of five books of poetry and regular editor, reviewer and contributor to many online and print magazines and writing collectives. Her work has been published in Rattle, Northern Poetry Review, Indiana Voice Journal, Trivia: Voices of Feminism and Memoryhouse Magazine among others. Daquin is of French/Egyptian heritage and her work reflects her experiences as a woman, lesbian and immigrant. www.thefeatheredsleep.com

Sarah Doughty: "Writing is a channel through which I attempt to heal. From my haunted past to my current, painful existence as the

result of Complex PTSD, debilitating migraines, and Fibromyalgia —
I try to be a beacon of hope for lost souls. My writing has been
featured in several anthologies. My poetry chapbook, *The Silence
Between Moonbeams*, and the acclaimed novels and novellas of the
Earthen Witch Universe, are always free."

Irma Do is a mother, runner, writer, partner, (social) worker, reader,
listener, crier, singer, eater, sleeper - not necessarily in that order
and usually, not all at the same time. She lives, out of her element, in
the wilds of central Pennsylvania. Her writings are infused with the
sweat and tears of an over the hill mother runner's race to make the
world better before passing it down to her children.

Michèle Duquet is a French-Canadian actor with a successful 40-
year international multi-lingual career in the film and TV industry.
Michèle is also a BioEnergy-Healing practitioner. Her writing has
been viewed over 400,000 times in her popular blog,
michelesorganics.wordpress.com. Michèle completed her first book
in 2018, a part memoir, part spiritual guide, where she shares the
profound metaphysical experiences she had in childhood and the
empowering human-soul lessons that came from them.

Aubrey Dunn is a wickedly clever writer. She gives voice to words,
mastering a brilliant uniqueness yet to be fully heard. Aubrey resides
in the Emerald City, "the World Capital of Coffee". Learn more
@www.hermourningcoffee.com

Matthew D. Eayre is a writer currently living in Louisville Kentucky.
His mission in life and as a writer is to be a positive influence on
anyone he encounters.

Tiffany Elliott is pursuing a Masters of Fine Arts in Creative Writing
at New Mexico State University. Her works explore issues of abuse,
trauma, and how recovery and resiliency allow people to remake

themselves. Her poetry has previously appeared in MUSE and Pacific Review.

Sabrina Escorcio was born to Italian immigrant parents in the Niagara region of Ontario, Canada. After years of journaling, poetry became an avenue of self-expression. This hunger for poetry was insatiable, scouring second hand book stores for more inspiration. There she found classic authors as well as many obscure poets, and began to transform journaling into the realm of confessional poetry.

Melissa Fadul teaches classical & contemporary poetry & advanced placement psychology in a public high school in New York. She lives with her wife, two bunnies and Maltese dog. Melissa also practices photography. She is working on a poetry manuscript and screenplay that she hopes Naomi Watts will read one day and want to turn into a film. Melissa can be contacted at: melissafadul@gmail.com

Deirdre Fagan is a widow, wife, and mother of two who has published poetry, fiction, and nonfiction in various online and print journals. Fagan is also the author to *Critical Companion to Robert Frost* and has published a number of critical essays on poetry, memoir, and teaching pedagogy. She teaches literature and writing at Ferris State University where she is also the Coordinator of Creative Writing. Meet her at deirdrefagan.com

Rachel Finch is a UK based writer that originally started using poetry as a way to accurately express herself after a number of traumatic experiences in her young life. She is the founder of the online community Bruised But Not Broken which was started with the purpose to raise awareness of abuse and trauma and to provide a place of comfort and support throughout the healing process.

Amanda J. Forrester received her MFA from the University of Tampa. Her poems have appeared or are forthcoming in Indolent Books' What Rough Beast, Collective Unrest, and the Sandhill

Review. She serves on the executive board of YellowJacket Press and snuggles with her fur babies when she isn't working long hours as a data analyst at Saint Leo University. Follow her on Twitter @ajforrester75.

Nicholas Gagnier is a Canadian writer and poet. He is the author of Leonard the Liar and Founding Fathers, as well as the creator of Free Verse Revolution, and co-founder of Blank Paper Press. Nicholas is an avid poet and his next release, All the Lonely People, will be available in 2019.

Nikita Goel is an out of the box thinker, award winning editor, writer and social media influencer with 23 books published worldwide. As a columnist for Different Truths and Editor for well-known publishing houses, she is recognized for her top-notch work with awards and certificates. Her Blog- " The Enchantress" holds a place in India's Top Blogs and her articles, poems and short stories are widely published in various online magazines, newspapers and websites. As a freelancer, she is her own boss and juggles between multiple jobs all over the world at the same time.

F.I. Goldhaber's words capture people, places, and events with a photographer's eye and a poet's soul. As a reporter, editor, business writer, and marketing communications consultant, they produced news stories, feature articles, editorial columns, and reviews for newspapers, corporations, governments, and non-profits in five states. Now paper, electronic, and audio magazines, books, newspapers, calendars, and street signs display their poetry, fiction, and essays, including more than 100 of their poems. http://www.goldhaber.net/

Joey Gould, a new *Sudden Denouement* member, is also a member of Mass Poetry involved in planning the Massachusetts Poetry Festival, teaching workshops in MA schools, & writing content for Masspoetry.org. His poetry appears on *Drunk Monkeys* (for which he also writes 100-word reviews), *District Lit*, *The Compassion Anthology*, *Memoir Mixtapes*, & more. He has performed with The Poetry Brothel & Shari Caplan's Poetry Circus.

Ali Grimshaw is the author of the blog, Flashlight Batteries, https://flashlightbatteries.blog/ She contributes to the world as an educator, dance teacher, coach and poet. Her poems have been published on Vita Brevis.

"My name is **N.R. Hart** (Nancy) and my first book of poetry "Poetry and Pearls" volume one was published in 2015, a collection of poetry and prose with poems about love, loss and heartbreak. My second book of poetry "Poetry and Pearls" volume two will be released this year, December 2018. I have been a romantic and an empath my whole life with an overwhelming need to help and heal others. My wish is to spread love, hope and positivity with my poetry."

S.L. Heaton: "Just a girl with some words and a pen that will always say it better than her mouth ever possibly could. She is on a journey to nowhere in particular and everywhere all at once, leaving bits of her soul along the way because silence will never be an option."

HLR is a 20-something prosetry writer from north London. Based on her own struggles with several mental illnesses, HLR writes creative non-fiction about a range of challenging subjects. With startling honesty and a sly injection of sardonic British droll, her gritty confessional style is one that can only be acquired through years of psychological anguish and too much time in the pub. Find more at www.treacleheart.com

Holly Rene Hunter is a native Floridian. She is a writer, artist, and a registered nurse. She began writing very young, at age eight, shortly after her mother passed away. She attended FSU and Barry University in Miami, Florida. She is an advocate for women's issues, racism, and bigotry.

Rachael Ikins is a 2016, 2018 Pushcart & 2013, 2018 CNY Book Award nominee and a 2018 Independent Book Award winner for Just Two Girls (Clare Songbirds Publishing House). She is a graduate of Syracuse University. Her multi genre/media work appears in worldwide journals. She is a member of NLAPW and Associated Artists of CNY and serves as the Associate Editor Clare Songbirds Publishing

Emily James is the pseudonym used by Lori Weyandt. Lori's soul roams from the mountains of Pennsylvania to the mountains of North Carolina. Her love of writing began as a teenager when she first started writing short stories. She shares her life with her fiancé Brian and daughter Kirsten.

Ashley Jane is an indie author from Alabama, where she lives with her husband and rescue cat named Shadow. She is a former Inmate Substance Abuse Counselor with research published in Crime and Delinquency magazine. She has also been featured on various poetry sites. Between editing, writing and consulting, you'll find her reading poetry books and psychological studies. Her first book, Love, Lies and Lullabies is now
available on Amazon.

This is **Rachel Kobin's** first published work. As the founder of the Philadelphia Writers Workshop, she helps others develop the full power of their voices. They, in turn, lift hers.

V.J. Knutson is a writer and blogger living in small town Ontario, Canada. A survivor of stranger abduction and rape, she is passionate not only about healing but also about lighting a way for her granddaughters and those to come. *One Woman's Quest* and *One Woman's Quest II* are her blogs.
Crystal Kinistino is a poet and lover of the written word. She has been previously published in Decanto Poetry Magazine. She blogs at

. She is inspired by such strong feminist writers as Virginia Woolf, Sylvia Plath, and Anne Sexton. She draws her inspiration from nature and life. She is a proud lesbian, radical feminist and half-blood Cree woman residing in the treaty #1 territory of Canada.

Jay Long is a New York based author, poet, and natural storyteller. His creative voice can be heard throughout social media and online writing communities. Through his writing and work with other writers, he continues to establish himself as one of today's prolific voices of modern poetry. To learn more about Jay and follow his writing journey, please visit jaylongwrites.com.

Katharine Love is a retired psychotherapist turned writer. She has just finished her first book, a memoir titled *The Lesbian Chronicles*. Katharine lives in Toronto with her circus puppy Lucille.

Lisa Low is a writer living in Connecticut. She spent 20 years as an English Professor. She was a TV theatre critic for CSB. She has published scholarly essays on Shakespeare, Ibsen; and Virginia Woolf; and an edited book from Cambridge UP on Milton and the Romantics. She has also published poems in a variety of places including Aphros, Phoebe, and Intro 11.

LM is an artist, writer, and activist.

Samantha Lucero of House San Francisco is a Midgard-born author and poet, First of her Name, The Indomitable, Undead Queen of the Black Lodge, Unseelie Bibliophile of the Black Forest, Veteran of The Valkyries, and Mother of Dragons. For more, visit sixredseeds.wordpress.com, or @sixredseeds on IG.

Julie A. Malsbury received her MA in Writing Students from Saint Joseph's University and teaches at various universities in the Philadelphia area. She lives with her husband and menagerie of 3 cats, 2 kittens, 2 dogs, and 1 snake—all rescues. In her spare time, she sings for social justice with the Anna Crusis, the longest running feminist choir in the United States.

Nandini Sen Mehra: "An army kid with a nomadic childhood, she eventually studied English Literature and went on to work in communication. She is a contributing editor for Creative Sparq, an online magazine and also a core member of The Rhyme Republic, a poetry group that celebrates a love for poetry and literature through events and poetry-related causes."

The writing of Indie Author, **Jamie Lynn Martin**, is as raw and diverse as the culture of her hometown, New Orleans, la. At age 7, Jamie began writing as a therapeutic outlet to express the emotions locked within. Even now she turns to ink for self-medicating. In addition to Jamie's upcoming debut book of poetry prose, her words have been featured in Cult Magazine and ail across social media.

Jessie Michelle is a lover of caffeine and words. She is and will forever be a hopeless romantic, but is learning that there are always two sides to every love story. Her work can be found on Instagram and Facebook. Her first book, "Conversations with the Moonlight" can be found on Amazon.

AmyKCM: "The bond we share as victims of assault is completely unacceptable, yet it unites and makes us irrepressible. Writing about my experience has taken a night that held dark memories and allowed me to find new hope and strength. I find happiness through writing and raising educated, aware and loving children. My rock (aka Husband) helped me reclaim my center and has shown me everlasting and enduring love."

Wilda Morris is Workshop Chair of Poets and Patrons of Chicago and Past President of the Illinois State Poetry Society. Her poems are found in numerous anthologies, webzines, and print publications, including *Li Poetry*, *Chaffin Journal and After Hours*. She has won awards for formal and free verse and haiku. Her book, tentatively titled *Pequod Poems: Gamming with Moby-Dick*, is due out next spring. Read her poetry blog at wildamorris.blogspot.com.

"My name is **Jack Neece** and I am a single parent of four beautiful children. I manage https://www.facebook.com/twistedmindletters/ and hope to spread healing and unity through my writing."

Lesléa Newman is the author of 70 books for readers of all ages including the poetry collections, I Carry My Mother, Lovely, and October Mourning: A Song for Matthew Shepard (novel-in-verse). She is the recipient of poetry fellowships from the National Endowment for the Arts and the Massachusetts Artists Foundation. A past poet laureate of Northampton, MA, she currently teaches at Spalding University's low-residency MFA in Writing program.

C. O'Mahony is the author of six publications. Her writing explores the evolution of human consciousness offering insight into authentic living. Inner harmony and wellbeing are themes running through her books. Visit www.colletteomahony.com for articles on evolving consciousness and more poetry and prose

Jesica Nodarse is a Cuban-born immigrant living in Florida, with her husband and children. A powerful writer and poet, an intense and driven woman, Jesica offers her unique perspective in today's world and empowers her friends and colleagues with passion and grace. She can be found on Facebook at facebook.com/heathenwordsmith and on Instagram at https://www.instagram.com/j.nodarse/ .

Georgia Park is a contributing editor of Sudden Denouement, founder of Whisper and the Roar, and author of Quit Your Job and Become a Poet (Out of Spite). She has been published in several literary magazines, most recently, The Offbeat. She does funny, playful, dark, morbid, Trump related and non-Trump related poems, with or without an emphasis on travel. Read more of her work at PrivateBadThoughts.com

Madame K Poetess is a poet who has turned the pain from her childhood, & from her experiences into a form of art through using words to connect with others, but also as a form of therapy for herself enabling her to heal & become the strong woman she is today, showing others that they too can make it out the other side, & rise from the fall.

Christine E. Ray is an indie author and freelance editor living outside of Philadelphia, Pennsylvania. Having served as Managing Editor of Sudden Denouement Publications and FVR Publishing, she founded Indie Blu(e) Publishing with Kindra M. Austin in September 2018. Her first book, *Composition of a Woman*, is available through Amazon and other major online book retailers. Read more of her work at https://braveandrecklessblog.com/.

Kristiana Reed is an English teacher and a writer (in her free time and day dreams.) She is the author of the WordPress blog My Screaming Twenties and she writes about love, her struggle with mental health, survival and hope. She is currently in the middle of producing Between the Trees, her debut anthology, and writing her first novel.

Hanlie Robbertse is an eternal student and teacher of life, hope, heartbreak and pain. As a writer and creator she aims to bring healing to not only herself but to others that may feel lost, heartbroken and alone. You can find her writing page on facebook at https://facebook.com/IamHanlie

Mary Rogers has dedicated her life to helping other others understand the phases of the moon and the cycles of nature while exploring the inner dimensions of their lives. Being Native American (Apsaalooke/Crow) and Korean, she fearlessly walks between worlds exploring the primal side of humanity while honoring each individual's sacred divinity. Passionate in all that she does, her favorite past time is getting naked on paper.

Michelle Schaper, from Western Australia, works supporting disabilities, (or as she says, 'enhancing people's abilities.') She is a mentor/advocate for mental health and domestic violence and has written poetry since her childhood. Michelle was attacked by two rapists aged fifteen and has survived violent relationships. You'll find more of Michelle's work on Facebook and Instagram and her books 'Soul Kissing' and 'Fairytale Bones' can be found at some online bookstores.

Carla Schwartz is a filmmaker, photographer, and blogger. Her poems have appeared in many journals and anthologies, including The Practicing Poet: Writing Beyond the Basics. Her second poetry collection is Intimacy with the Wind, Finishing Line Press (2017). Her debut collection is Mother, One More Thing, (Turning Point, 2014). Her CB99videos youtube channel has 1,900,000+ views. Learn more at carlapoet.com, or wakewiththesun.blogspot.com or find her on twitter or instagram @cb99videos.

Tanya Shukla is a high school teacher and a published author. She holds a master's degree in English Literature and Linguistics and is an avid reader of classics. She published her first anthology of poems; *A Wind's Tale* in 2017 and is now working on her second book of poetry. She currently resides in Connecticut, with her young daughter and husband.

Raney Simmon is 25 years-old and a Columbia College graduate with a Bachelor of Arts degree in Writing for Print and Digital Media. She owns a blog on WordPress called *Rainy Day's Books, Video Games and Other Writings* where she mostly writes book reviews, but talks about other subjects as well such as video games and occasionally writes her own poems.

Robin Anna Smith is a non-binary, disabled writer and visual artist residing in Wilmington, Delaware. She primarily writes about personal experiences with trauma, disability, mental health, and gender identity. Her work appears in a variety of journals and anthologies internationally. More can be found at her website robinannasmith.com and Twitter @robinannasmith.

Mary Hansen lives in the Fortuna Foothills of Yuma, Arizona with her husband Keith. She enjoys playing piano and singing, painting with acrylics, and writing. She has previously published poetry in an anthology. Mary has three grown children and two grandchildren, loves the desert after a rain, and gets excited at the smell of hot cocoa on a blustery day.

Megha Sood lives in New Jersey, USA. She is a contributing author/editor at GoDogGO, Candles Online, Free Verse Revolution, Whisper and the Roar and Poets Corner. Her works have appeared in Visual Verse, Vita Brevis,521 magazine, KOAN(Paragon press), Fourth and Sycamore, Dime Show Review, and coming up Piker Press etc. She won 1st prize in NAMI NJ Axelrod Mental Health Poetry contest. She blogs at https://meghasworldsite.wordpress.com/.

Christie L. Starkweather: "Since the age of twelve, writing has been a major component of who I am. In 2017, I decided to share my work with the world by starting CLS Poetry by Christie Starkweather on Facebook, because I wanted people to know they were not alone in their struggles. With all struggle comes strength, and by fighting together, we are unstoppable."

Ann Stolinsky is the founder and owner of Gontza Games, an independent board and card game company. Her website is www.gontzagames.com. She is also a partner in Gemini Wordsmiths, a full-service copyediting and content creating company. Visit www.geminiwordsmiths.com for more information and testimonials. Several of her stories have been published in the last few years.

Eric Syrdal is a poet/author. He's an avid gamer and Sci-Fi enthusiast. He enjoys reading science fiction and fantasy literature and spends a great deal of his writing time focused in those genres. He is a romantic, at heart. His work usually contains elements of the supernatural and fantastic along with potent female voices and archetypes. He is from New Orleans, Louisiana, where he lives with his wife and two children.

Petru J Viljoen: "A survivor of emotional and physical abuse I found my voice and true nature through art and writing. The psyche is strengthened through creative processes which aids the healing process considerably. Mainstream society continues to try and silence victims of abuse but by insisting on being heard the same society is conscientized."

My name is **Angie Waters** a.k.a **A. Shea**. I am a survivor of childhood/adult sexual abuse and trauma. My work often reflects my own healing process. Writing has allowed me to connect with others with similar experiences, find meaning in my own trials and provide me with a renewed sense of purpose and self worth. I am grateful to be a part of this anthology that will help spread awareness and healing.

Marcia J. Weber is both a survivor and a healer, having worked for over 2 decades with survivors of various ilks. Her writing was born in great measure as the unstoppable outpouring of pain and recover. She believes passionately in the need to speak ones truths. She writes as Aurora Phoenix at Insights from "Inside"

Carrie Weis is a painter and writer. She works full time as the Museum and Gallery Director for Ferris State University. Carrie has also assisted with the creation of exhibitions and displays that address topics such as racism and sexism through the Jim Crow Museum of Racist Memorabilia and the Museum of Sexist Objects at FSU.

Rachael Westwood: "Mother of five, amateur photographer, deep thinker, shy singer, life long writer of words in my mind which are patiently awaiting pen and paper."

Lola White's poems have appeared in a variety of literary magazines and a book, "The Seed at Center." In the 1990's she produced a poetry program for the Nashville, (TN) "Talking Library," presenting such diverse authors and poets as Philip Levine, Ann Patchett, Bill Brown, Jeff Hardin and A Manette Ansay reading from their work. Ms. White is a photographer as well as a poet. She lives and works in Nashville, TN.

Melita White is founder and writer of the blog Feminist Confessional, a space that features feminist poetry, essays and personal pieces in a confessional style, with a focus on the MeToo movement. She is a composer and musician and has worked in academia.

R.S. Williams: "I write strange and provocative things, usually from multiple perspectives—human and otherwise. I have an increasingly codependent relationship with words and started writing them down as a way to get even closer to them. I love them, they tolerate me— and we happily use each other like porn stars. P.S. I have a really bizarre sense of humor. Like. Really."

Laurie D. Wise is an artist and writer from Oregon. She has several poems featured in the Sudden Denouement Literary Collective, Anthology Volume 1 and Free Verse Revolution, Swear to Me. Wise began writing as a blogger at A Lion Sleeps in the Heart of the Brave and is a contributing writer at Sudden Denouement Literary Collective, Blood into Ink and Whisper and the Roar.

Rachel Woolf lives and works in the Philadelphia area. She slays dragons, takes care of her amazing kids, and occasionally finds time to write poetry, nonfiction and memoir. This is her first published piece in a long time. She thanks her boyfriend for encouraging her to write and submit this poem. She chose a pen name so that other members of her family can tell their own stories.

April Yvette is a widow, survivor, warrior and author. She writes of grief and tragedy framed by the beauty of love, hope and dreams. From highs to lows, this woman's soul is inked onto paper.

Sally Zakariya's poetry has appeared in some 75 journals and been nominated for the Pushcart Prize and Best of the Net. Her chapbook *The Unknowable Mystery of Other People* is forthcoming from the Poetry Box. She is also the author of *Personal Astronomy, When You Escape, Insectomania,* and *Arithmetic and other verses*, as well as the editor of a poetry anthology, *Joys of the Table*. Zakariya blogs at www.butdoesitrhyme.com.

Sources for Merril D. Smith's Foreword

Clinton Foundation and Bill & Melinda Gates Foundation. 2015. "No Ceilings: The Full Participation Report." Accessed August 31, 2017. http://www.noceilings.org/.

Fang. Marina. 2018. "National Sexual Assault Hotline Had Busiest Day in its History After Kavagnaugh." *Huffington Post.* October 1. Accessed October 11, 2018. https://www.huffingtonpost.com/entry/rainn-national-sexual-assault-hotline_us_5bb20b91e4b027da00d54b3c

Ford, Christine Blasey. 2018. "Prepared Statement for the Judiciary Committee." *New York Times.* September 26. Accessed October 11, 2018. https://www.nytimes.com/2018/09/26/us/politics/christine-blasey-ford-prepared-statement.html?module=inline

James, S. E., Herman, J. L., Rankin, S., Keisling, M., Mottet, L., & Anafi, M. (2016). *The Report of the 2015 U.S. Transgender Survey.* Washington, DC: National Center for Transgender Equality.

Miller, Hayley. 2018. "C-SPAN Callers Recall Their Own Sexual Assaults After Christine Blasey Ford's Testimony. *Huffington Post.* September 27. Accessed October 11, 2018. https://www.huffingtonpost.com/entry/cspan-caller-christine-blasey-ford_us_5bacfd89e4b0425e3c21268c?dvn

Murphy, Heather. 2018. "Expecting Women to Describe How Sexual Assault Affected Them Creates Barrier to Reporting It." *New York Times.* September 27. Accessed October 11, 2018. https://www.nytimes.com/2018/09/27/health/dr-ford-sexual-assault.html?module=inline

NISIVS. N.d. "NISVS: An Overview of 2010 Findings on Victimization by Sexual Orientation." National Intimate Partner and Sexual

Violence Survey. Accessed October 20, 2018.
https://www.cdc.gov/violenceprevention/pdf/cdc_nisvs_victimization_final-a.pdf

Pellegrini, Gianina. 2018. "Sexual Victimization of Men and Boys." In *Encyclopedia of Rape and Sexual Violence.* Edited by Merril D. Smith, 354-380. Santa Barbara, CA: ABC-CLIO.

RAINN. 2018. Criminal Justice System: Statistics." Rape, Abuse & Incest National Network (RAINN). Accessed October 20, 2018. https://www.rainn.org/statistics/criminal-justice-system

RAINN. 2018. "Scope of the Problem: Statistics." Rape, Abuse & Incest National Network (RAINN). Accessed October 20, 2018. https://www.rainn.org/statistics/scope-problem

Smith, Merril D. 2018. "Stranger Rape." In *Encyclopedia of Rape and Sexual Violence.* Edited by Merril D. Smith, 429-452. Santa Barbara, CA: ABC-CLIO.

UN Women. 2017. "Facts and Figures: Ending Violence Against Women." Accessed October 20, 2018. http://www.unwomen.org/en/what-we-do/ending-violence-against-women/facts-and-figures#notes

Leading the National Effort to End Sexual Violence

National Sexual Assault Hotline

RAINN created and operates the National Sexual Assault Hotline, which has helped more than 2.5 million people since 1994. The hotline is available by phone (800.656.HOPE) and online chat in English (online.rainn.org) and Spanish (rainn.org/es). The service is free, confidential, and available 24/7.

Call

When someone calls 800.656.HOPE, they will be connected with a RAINN support specialist or a local center from RAINN's network of more than 1,000 sexual assault service providers throughout the country. Staff offer advice, information, and support. In some areas, providers can offer additional local services, such as hospital accompaniment. Together, RAINN and these local providers are able to operate the hotline 24/7 to provide confidential support to survivors and their friends and family.

Chat

Talking about what happened can be an important part of moving forward and seeking help, but not everyone is comfortable talking over the phone. Survivors and loved ones can access help online (online.rainn.org) through a chat-based platform on a computer, phone, or tablet. RAINN's staff provides support to thousands of survivors each month, many of whom are disclosing the experience for the first time.

Help for the Military Community

RAINN created and operates the DoD Safe Helpline, a crisis support service for members of the military community affected by sexual assault. Safe Helpline provides live, confidential, anonymous support and information. Members of the DoD community can access Safe Helpline online (safehelpline.org), over the phone (877-995-5247), through a self-care app, and through a group chat service (safehelproom.org).

Made in the USA
Middletown, DE
05 December 2018